CONTEM
GREEK T...

Volume 1

The Parade
Loula Anagnostaki

Love Thriller
George Skourtis

With Power from Kifissia
Dimitris Kehaidis and Eleni Haviara

ARCADIA BOOKS
LONDON

Arcadia Books Ltd
15–16 Nassau Street
London WIN 7RE

First published in the United Kingdom 1999
Copyright © Loula Anagnostaki, George Skourtis, Dimitris
Kehaidis and Eleni Haviara 1999

ISBN 1–900850–28–1

Typeset in Monotype Plantin by Discript, London WC2N 4BL
Printed in the United Kingdom by Cromwell Press, Trowbridge, Wiltshire

This book has been published with the support of

HELLENIC   THE HELLENIC
FOUNDATION   FOUNDATION
FOR CULTURE

Arcadia Books distributors are as follows:

in the UK and elsewhere in Europe:
Turnaround Publishers Services
Unit 3, Olympia Trading Estate
Coburg Road
London N22 6TZ

in the USA and Canada:
Consortium Book Sales and Distribution, Inc.
1045 Westgate Drive
St Paul, MN 55114–1065

in Australia:
Tower Books
PO Box 213
Brookvale, NSW 2100

in New Zealand:
Addenda
Box 78224
Grey Lynn
Auckland

in South Africa:
Peter Hyde Associates (Pty) Ltd
PO Box 2856
Cape Town 8000

The Parade

by

Loula Anagnostaki

Translated by
Anastasia Revi and Yiorgos Glastras

The Characters

ZOE.
Twenty-three.

ARIS.
Seventeen.

A room with old wallpaper. A door narrow and tall.
The furniture: two beds reminiscent of old iron beds with bars;
one is dishevelled. A rocking chair. A stool. A shelf. Bookcases.
There is no proper window. Only something like a vent, high
up, with no bars but glass that opens.
There are lots of paper boats and planes on the floor, table, stool
and dishevelled bed; as well as many books and maps scattered
about the room. It's dark. Pause. Out of the darkness drums are
heard; then marching music; sometimes heard together; some-
times on their own; sometimes near; sometimes in the distance.
Pause. Light.
As the light comes up a sound of a trumpet is heard in the
distance; it's as if the musician is trying to find a tune. At the
same time and place a drummer seems to be rehearsing.
ZOE *is seen, sitting in the rocking chair, facing the audience. She*
knits rhythmically, singing softly.

ZOE: [SONG]

ARIS *enters. He is thoughtful. He fidgets with a chair, he climbs*
onto a crate and glances out of the vent. The trumpet and the
drums sound in the background. He walks round the room
fidgeting with the chain. He throws the chain on the table. He
lies on the floor and starts to cut his paper ships in order to play
'battle ships'. After placing his ships in a battle position he takes
an aeroplane in each hand the flies them over the fleet firing. All
that time ZOE *hasn't stopped her knitting or singing.*

ZOE: [SONG]
ZOE: Ari, are we alone?
ARIS: (*mimics the sound of the plane*) Yes.
ZOE: Father has left.
ARIS: He has. (*He fires.*) [SOUNDS]

ZOE: I didn't hear the door bang. There's that noise coming from the square. Shut the window.

What is it? Trumpets?

ARIS: Mmm. (*He stands up and closes the window begrudgingly.*)

ZOE: And drums yes?

The parade will definitely take place in front of our house, I'm sure. A street festival – a celebration – maybe?

ARIS: If you'd bothered to look at the diary you would have seen that today is a holiday.

ZOE: A national holiday with banners and flags. And the school children passing under the balconies.

Are there lots of people gathered in the square?

ARIS: No, no one's turned up yet. (*He takes three small balls from the dishevelled bed and throws them up and down trying to mimic a juggler.*)

ZOE: I don't like the parade. Do you remember when I was young and I stayed out in the sun far too long and I ended up with terrible sunstroke and I was vomiting and I almost died?

ARIS: It was not during the parade but when we went swimming, at the seaside.

ZOE: Do you remember?

ARIS: No, I was very young. Maybe I wasn't even born. (*He is trying with the balls but not succeeding.*)

ZOE: Anyway, it doesn't matter.

(*Short pause*)

ZOE: What did Father put on today?

ARIS: His blue jacket.

ZOE: The same one he was wearing yesterday? The third button from the bottom is missing and the side lining is all ripped. I was meaning to sew it first thing this morning. Now that I mention it I think I did sew it after all.

ARIS: (*has finally managed to juggle*) You didn't. There were only two buttons.

ZOE: And you let him leave like that? Did he put on his jumper at least?

ARIS: He did.

ZOE: The yellow or the grey?

ARIS: The yellow.

ZOE: The yellow is warmer. It's getting chilly outside.

ARIS: How do you know?

ZOE: How do I know what? (*During the conversation she hasn't looked at him at all.*)

ARIS: (*discards the balls. He stands bored against the wall, puts his hands in his pockets.*) That the weather has got worse.

ZOE: (*still knitting*) Father told me last night when he came. He told me 'You should wear your black shawl. It's autumn'. And then he breathed on his fingers and said 'We should light the stove soon'.
He's been feeling the cold recently.
He's already asked me for woollen blankets and ordered me to bring him hot tea before going to bed.
Maybe he is sick. What do you think, is he sick?

ARIS: (*climbs up to the window and opens the glass*) No, I don't think so.

ZOE: What's happening out there?

ARIS: Nothing yet. The square is empty.

ZOE: Are the shops closed?

ARIS: All shut up with the shutters down.

ZOE: Is anyone sitting on the benches?

ARIS: I'm telling you, the place is absolutely deserted. Nobody's arrived yet.

ZOE: So, where's the music coming from?

ARIS: It must be from far away. I can't tell. But, they'll arrive any minute now. I'm sure the parade is going to pass right in front of the house.

ZOE: Why are you so sure?

ARIS: (*closes the glass and without stepping down from the crate he faces* ZOE) They have placed a statue in the square right in the middle. It seems they'll unveil the statue of a hero for the anniversary.

ZOE: Which hero? Didn't you see?

ARIS: No. It's covered with a white cloth, you can't see anything.

ZOE: Then how do you know it's a statue?

ARIS: What else could it be? They've put it on a high pedestal which is surrounded by a rope barrier that people can stand behind to watch the parade. (*With sudden joy*) It's crystal clear, they are coming in a few minutes.

ZOE: (*singing*) [SONG]

(ARIS*'s enthusiasm wanes. He steps down slowly and stands behind* ZOE.)

ARIS: Are you singing?

ZOE: Am I? I haven't noticed. I was day-dreaming.

ARIS: What were you thinking?

ZOE: I'm not thinking. I'm knitting.

ARIS: What are you knitting? No, don't tell me. I'll guess myself. You're knitting something for yourself. A shawl?

ZOE: No, you're wrong.

ARIS: Then ... a cardigan.

ZOE: No, not a cardigan. I knitted one last week.

ARIS: A sleeveless jumper.

ZOE: No, no, no. A whole dress. Here's the skirt.

ARIS: Anyway, it is something for you. At least, I got that right.

ZOE: You did. But I think you asked me yesterday as well, and I told you.

ARIS: Can I look at it?

ZOE: (*shows him*) Isn't it beautiful?

ARIS: It's wonderful. Maroon! That's the name of the colour. Just a bit small for you.

ZOE: But I'm very slim.

ARIS: Small and long.

ZOE: But I'm tall. It will be perfect for me.

ARIS: You're short.

ZOE: You don't know what you're talking about. You say that because you're bullying me. You always want to bully me.

ARIS: Short and fat.

ZOE: You're mean. I'm not talking to you.

ARIS: In this house there's no big mirror. Well, you've never seen yourself in full length. Short and fat. That's what you

are and you don't know it. (*He jumps around.*)
I have a sister short and plump.

ZOE: I won't speak to you again. Give it back to me! (*She tries to grab the knitting back but* ARIS *leaps away from her.*)

ARIS: Short and dumpy (*Sings*) Legs like pegs.

ZOE: (*chases him*) Liar! Liar! Give it back now.

ARIS: (*running*) The dress is minute, it's useless. (*He rolls it into a ball and throws it across the room still singing.*) Nose like a crow's. (*She chases him around the room and each time* ZOE *gets close to the dress* ARIS *is fast and throws it away and steps on it.*)

ZOE: Let go, let go, let go.

ARIS: Here they are.

(*From the time she started chasing him, the noise of a crowd and approaching band music have started. Now, the noise has become quite loud and* ARIS *notices it suddenly. He leaves the dress and runs to the window leaving* ZOE *crying on the floor.*)

ARIS: They've already arrived. The square is full, is almost full – listen! They're coming from everywhere, they're taking up positions behind the ropes.
Some of them are all dressed up for the parade, others look like shit – stop it, stop crying, come and see. You act like a child. They're opening up their umbrellas to keep the sun off; umbrellas for the sun, it's silly isn't it? Stop crying, you make me angry.
Some of them have made peaked hats out of newspaper. Ah! They've got the best idea! They're tying a knot at each end of their bandannas to make a hat which the wind can't blow away. The middle of the square is empty. The army hasn't arrived yet, neither have the schools. It's only the children from the orphanage playing the music.

(*He turns to* ZOE *who's returned to her chair and has taken up her knitting again grumpily. He closes the window slowly. Steps down and approaches her.*)

ARIS: Are you angry with me?

(ZOE *moves her chair making it very obvious how she feels.*)

ARIS: Listen: tomorrow I'll tell Father to buy turquoise coloured wool for you to knit another dress. This colour looks cheap don't you see? (*Pause*) But then again, what do I know – I'm a man. I have no idea about colours. But, to be honest, a turquoise coloured dress with ... with a bit of gold on the collar? Wouldn't it be beautiful. You have to admit that my idea about the gold is brilliant! (*Pause*) You're not talking to me? All right I will keep my mouth shut for one whole day. (*He goes back to his ships.*) Do you hear me? A whole day. Not a single word. [SOUNDS] (*He plays.*)

ZOE: (*nastily*) When I sit here on my chair knitting and you ask me again and again what do I think, do you really want to know?

ARIS: [SOUNDS] (*He fires.*)

ZOE: (*continues with the same attitude*) I think how happy I would be if I had a sister instead of you. I am so unlucky not to have a sister.

ARIS: [SOUNDS] (*He dive bombs.*)

ZOE: This room is horrible. I can't look at it. Your ships, your footballs, your maps, your books thrown everywhere. I feel like grabbing and burning them.

ARIS: Well, then I'll set fire to your knitting basket. Actually, I won't burn all your knitting completely. I'll just leave it scorched so you'll see it and explode!

ZOE: I know you very well. You're quite capable of doing it. You're mean and dirty. Your bed smells. You never make your bed. Do you know what any sister's bed would be like.

ARIS: [SOUNDS]

ZOE: Covered with a feather eiderdown, pink feather eiderdown and white pillow cases with pale blue ribbons and I would knit a thick yellow rug to put under her feet before they touch the floor.

I wouldn't let anyone else come in here. It would just be the two of us, just the two of us. We would talk and talk

... I would tell her all my secrets.

ARIS: Do you have secrets?

ZOE: Of course I have. But I'll never reveal them to you because you're a man.

ARIS: Not even a little bit?

ZOE: (*shakes her head in a negative way*) Not even a little bit.

(ARIS *stands up and starts walking round her.*)

ARIS: Then, I won't tell you anything about mine either. (*He looks at her surreptitiously.*) For instance, I'll tell you nothing about the key.

ZOE: The key ... which key?

ARIS: (*goes to the door and unlocks the key from above it*) This one! (*He holds it in front of her face.*)

ZOE: That's the front door key.

ARIS: Exactly. It's the front door key. One day I'll take it and I'll go out. (*He looks towards the window.*) I'll go down to the harbour.

ZOE: What will you do at the harbour?

ARIS: I'll watch the ships. I'll choose a day when the navy will be here to see a real battleship.

ZOE: How do you know when that day will be?

ARIS: I'll hear the cannon shots. You can hear them from here. Well, when I hear them I'll know and I'll leave. Then, I might go for a walk in the park.

ZOE: There's no park.

ARIS: Who told you?

ZOE: I did. To get to this house – I remember it very well – we walked through the whole city and we didn't pass through any park.

ARIS: Maybe. It doesn't matter. However, I didn't tell you the most important thing.

ZOE: The most important thing?

ARIS: (*conspiratorially and triumphantly*) I'll go to the cinema which is around the back. I will get a ticket and I'll go in.

ZOE: How do you know there's a cinema back there? You haven't told me. Tell me, how do you know?

ARIS: I know it because I discovered it all by myself. (*The same way as before*) For a week now, every night at ten and twelve o'clock people burst out of the square, a lot of people, crowds of people. They go by our window and spread out along the narrow passages. All those people must come out from somewhere. Well, after thinking about it for a long time, I realized that they cannot come out from anywhere else except that cinema which's just been built round here. If you weren't asleep by eight you would have seen them too. But, it's foolish of me to tell you all these things. (*In a mysterious tone*) From now on not even a word.

ZOE: Then I won't tell you anything I plan to do either . . . I won't tell you anything about that day.

ARIS: Which day?

ZOE: The day the square will be absolutely empty, deserted, because it will be Sunday morning and the shops will be closed. Everyone would be gone from the previous night, the fruit-sellers, the poultry-sellers, the gypsies selling carpets and the people selling bread rolls. It will be cold and no one will come to sit on the benches.

ARIS: And then, then?

ZOE: Then what?

ARIS: You said it will be Sunday morning.

ZOE: (*slowly and mysteriously*) Then I'll open the door and I'll go out. I'll walk around the square, right round it, I'll go past in front of the carts and the crates and the benches and the church and in front of the shops which sell copper handicrafts, casseroles, pots and pans, everything made of red copper polished like gold.

(*Pause.* ARIS *goes to the window, thoughtful.*)

ARIS: Why are they so late?

ZOE: Has the army arrived?

ARIS: Not yet. (*He takes his juggling balls again and makes a nervous attempt.*)

ZOE: Ari.

ARIS: Yes.

ZOE: What I just told you.

ARIS: Yes.

ZOE: I won't do it. (*Stops throwing the balls*) Because the square is never empty for a long time. Listen, I timed how long it takes to walk right round it. At least a quarter of an hour if I walk fast and half an hour if I go very slowly. I noticed – with a watch in my hand – that within that quarter or that half hour there is always someone to pass by there even if it's Sunday, even if it's very cold or freezing.

ARIS: Maybe you timed it wrong. Do you want us to time it again together?

ZOE: No, I'm sure I did the right thing. There's always some passer-by. Except during the night. But at night it's dark.

ARIS: Are you afraid of the dark?

ZOE: Very. Haven't you noticed that?

ARIS: Yes.

ZOE: I've been afraid since that night I went out with father.

ARIS: Which time? I don't remember. You've never told me about it.

ZOE: It's been a long time now … years maybe. We had just moved here. We left you asleep. We went out, just the two of us. It was very windy and rainy. We were walking and walking. I didn't have a clue where we were going. All the streets looked the same to me. I couldn't see a thing. Such a deep darkness … Not a light in sight and the houses all shut up, windows shut, no light. (*Sighs and carries on*) Father was looking for someone, that's what I sensed. We knocked at four – five doors but no one opened. Finally we reached a clearing, no houses, nothing. We stopped. 'Here,' father said 'we'll wait for him.' Then I realized that it had got even darker … pitch black. I searched and found his hand and I held it tight because I was really scared and suddenly (*Touches her neck*) … suddenly I was hit by a terrifying idea. What if the hand I was holding was not father's hand but somebody else's, a stranger's … and I got even more scared and I was shaking in case dawn was breaking. And it was raining … raining (*She hides her face in her hands.*)

(*Small pause*)

ARIS: You have never told me about it.

ZOE: (*uncovering her face*) No.

ARIS: (*walking around*) Then I have to tell you. I won't do the things I told you about.

ZOE: You won't go down to the harbour for the ships?

ARIS: No.

ZOE: And the battle ship?

ARIS: No. I won't go to the cinema either. And do you know why? Because the very same night that I thought about all these, I had a dream.

ZOE: A dream? I never dream. I have no dreams.

ARIS: I dreamt that I took the key (*Shows her the key*) and opened the door. The front door (*He describes the story vividly with gestures.*) But, behind it no pavement or square, instead a large furnished room.

ZOE: What kind of furniture was there?

ARIS: There was a big sideboard up to the ceiling. In the middle a long narrow table, very big with twelve chairs around it. The table had a maroon cloth and the chairs had the same colour upholstery. And there was also a big window that took up almost the whole wall and in front of it hung a large maroon curtain. At the end of the room there was a door. And in the lock, there was a key ... Without even realizing how, I opened that door and...

ZOE: And?

ARIS: I was in another room the same as the previous one, only this one was much bigger than the first except the sideboard was missing and in the empty space the wall was bleached.

ZOE: So, there was just the big table and the chairs.

ARIS: Yes and the big maroon curtain covering the whole window. And opposite there was again a door and a key in the lock.

ZOE: And did you open that too?

ARIS: I did and there was a third room, an even bigger one than the previous two and the table in the middle was on its own; the chairs with the maroon upholstery were missing now. Just the curtain and the window and the door at the end with the key. I open it and now the room is empty, completely empty and twice as big as the square. More than that: three to four times as big and only the curtain was still hanging at the window and the door with the key at the end – the door, you got it?

ZOE: (*scared and carried away*) No.

ARIS: Don't you understand? In the next room the curtain itself would also be missing. There would be only the window and behind the window ... I screamed and I woke up. Do you understand now?

ZOE: No, I don't.

ARIS: (*rubs his face unconsciously*) Yes, maybe you're right. What's there to understand? I think that ... it was a stupid dream. Yes, now that I've described it, I can see, it was silly.

ZOE: You have never told me about it either.

ARIS: We don't talk a lot the two of us, do we? On the other hand we've got no one else but each other. There's just the two of us.

ZOE: There's not just the two of us, there's father too. There's three of us in this house (*Counts her knitting stitches*) ... one ... two ... three ... (*She continues her counting, humming.*)

ARIS: Yes, but he's out all day and when he comes back he goes straight to bed. At times it feels to me we're strangers to him, a burden. And you?

ZOE: Fifteen ... sixteen.

ARIS: You? ... I'm asking you.

ZOE: Twenty seven ... eight. Leave me alone. I'm counting, don't you see?

ARIS: Every night I go to his room and I watch him getting ready to go to bed. I know it upsets him. I see him trying to be quicker. I sit there on purpose and look at him taking off his jacket, his shirt, his trousers. He folds them carefully, he puts on his pyjamas, lies on the bed, pulling the sheet up to his chin ... I watch everything, everything,

nothing escapes me. And then 'Switch off the light' he
says to me and I switch it off and I go out.

That's it. He never talks to me, he never says anything.
Once when he was away I was like a maniac. I started
searching around his room turning everything upside
down. The drawers, the wardrobes, the mattresses, the
pillows. I turned all his pockets inside out, I even searched
his shoes, his slippers but I didn't find anything. Why did
I do it? ... just because! Except a picture, I kept it, I
didn't put it back in its place. It must be old because it's
yellow at the edges and he's very young in it. He has a
beard, such a long beard. He's sitting on a rock looking at
the sea. (*Pause*) Tell me, did you ever consider that he
might not be our father? I'm asking you something ...
why don't you answer.

(ZOE *continues counting just by moving her lips now.*)

ARIS: Have you ever thought of that? I have. Yes. Many
times. Well ... say something. Why don't you speak? I'm
asking you. (*Screams next to her ear.* ZOE *annoyed jerks
away from him.*) Well do you know what else?

I've even thought that you might not be my sister. Why
should you be anyway? We don't look alike. Should I
bring the mirror so that we can look at ourselves side by
side? Besides, you're six years older than me and I should
remember you from way back, because younger brothers
remember their older sisters. I don't remember you at all.
I don't remember you at the age of ten, nor at twelve, nor
at fifteen, but much later, much later. Do you hear what
I'm saying? (*Screams*) Won't you answer? Come on,
speak, speak. The silence in here drives me nuts. (*Screams
loudly just like Tarzan*) [SOUNDS] (*With his hands round his
mouth like savages. Suddenly he jumps on* ZOE *and holds her
head.*) Let me check if you've been a good girl today!
Have you cleaned your ears?

ZOE: (*tries to escape from him*) Leave me alone.

ARIS: Show me your nails.

ZOE: No. (*Her knitting almost drops from her hands.*)

ARIS: You'd better tell me you've done the homework I set
you. Lazy cow. Let's see if you know much about
geography. How many states are there in South America?
Zero! Asia? Zero! What is made in Chile? Tell me. Zero.
Zero. History now: when did Napoleon live? When did
Robespierre live? How many Ludovicks were there in
France? Who was the first king of the Greeks? Who killed
Abraham Lincoln? Zero, zero, zero. (*All that time he spins
her chair around.*) Mathematics now: quickly 127 times
213 quickly, quickly . . . multiply . . . not ready yet?

ZOE: (*bursts out manically*) Leave me alone.

My head, my poor head. (*She pushes him strongly and
throws him on the floor.*)

(ARIS *stands up.*)

ARIS: I'll leave you alone, if you promise that we'll stand
and watch the parade together.

ZOE: (*stubbornly*) No. (*He takes her knitting again.*)

ARIS: But it should be starting any minute now. It's your
loss. (*He has gone to the window.*) Hey, hey! Look how
many people there are. They're coming. There's no end
to them.

They're crowding behind the ropes and waiting. I think
that the army and the schools will arrive together. They'll
seep in from everywhere. The square will be full. So? Will
you stand here with me and watch?

ZOE: (*sharply*) I don't like the parade.

ARIS: You're so stubborn. I like it. I think it's the only thing
I like.

ZOE: The crowd pushes you.

Do you remember when I was almost bulldozed? Do you
remember?

ARIS: It wasn't at the parade, stupid. There was bombing,
we were running to the shelters. And don't ask me all the
time if I remember this or if I remember that. I don't
remember anything. I was very young. Ah! if only it would
start. This was my favourite day when I was at school. I used
to look forward to growing up and being the flag-bearer. I

prayed to my body to get tall, six feet tall, so they would
make me the flag-bearer. But here I am – I stayed short. It's
a pity isn't it? Mmm ... listen, listen to the drums. (*He
watches.*) They're still far away. I'd be in high school now. I
might have been a drummer. You never know. You don't
have to be tall to be a drummer. (*He taps rhythmically on
the table, an accompaniment to his words.*) Parara, pararam
... pararam ... Should I show you something? (*Runs to
his dishevelled bed, bends down, pulls out a box from under it
and amongst other things finds a school cap. He looks at it in
awe and then puts it on his head.*) A cap!

ZOE: Where did you find it?

ARIS: I've kept it for years. I wear it on national holidays.

ZOE: I haven't seen it before.

ARIS: You have but you don't remember, you never
remember anything, except your own things. (*Walks up
and down mimicking a drummer*) Pararam ... Pararam ...
I stole it from a senior when I was at primary school ...
[DRUM SOUND] ... Zoe, shall I tell you a secret? (*Goes
towards her and leans in*) If you wanted, it you cared just a
little for me, I could tell you all my secrets. Well, the guy
I stole the cap from lives near us, I've seen him often
passing the square. I mean ... I'm almost sure it's him.
Sometimes I feel like opening the window and calling him
but I don't know his name. I call him my friend, that's
what I call him, because I don't know his real name. Of
course he wouldn't even notice me, he's much older than
me. He'd be around twenty eight now and tall, six feet tall,
six feet six inches tall. I'll point him out to you some day.
You'll like him, I'm sure.

ZOE: I don't like men.

ARIS: And he'll like you too. You know you're not ugly at
all. You've got a beautiful neck. It's just that you keep it
covered up. If you put your hair up it would be better.
Shall we try a new look? I'll do it for you.

ZOE: Don't dare touch my hair.

ARIS: You've got beautiful eyes too and a beautiful fore-
head. So, do you want me to show him to you?

ZOE: No.

ARIS: (*gets angry*) You're so stubborn. Stubborn and mean. And indifferent and deaf, yes, deaf. I talk to you and you don't answer. You're just like father. I do everything I can to please you. I've made four baskets for your knitting and you don't like any of them. Do you know how difficult it is to make a basket? My fingers bleed ... I go through the same thing with father. No matter what I do he doesn't pay me the slightest attention. Do you want to know what happened this morning? I went to his room, stood behind him and watched him getting ready to go out. He didn't talk to me, he acted as if I wasn't there. Finally I said: 'It's the parade today'. Not a word from him. He gets his yellow jumper and puts it on. I say to him louder: 'It's the parade today'. Silence. 'It'll be here in the square'. (*Pause. Loudly*) 'They've brought the statue'. He put on his jacket, he would have left the room in two steps, and at that moment, I don't know what happened to me but I started crying and screaming. I collapsed. I was screaming 'the parade will take place'.

And I was rolling until I heard the door shut and his foot steps go down the stairs ...

ZOE: You should be ashamed, a man of your age crying and scrambling about the floor ... You make me sick...

ARIS: I know ... I make you sick ... I'm disgusting. Because I'm ugly eh? (*He takes a mirror.*) And short ... and silly ... I have fat lips (*He stretches his lips in a coarse fashion.*) big nose ... (*Pulls faces*) small eyes, straight hair ...

(*From the time he looked at the mirror, making funny faces, marching music is heard in the background.* ZOE *starts singing.*)

ZOE: [SONG]

(*The marching music is getting louder and* ARIS *tries to listen. The last verse can't be heard because of the music and* ARIS *has jumped up to the window.*)

ARIS: (*excited*) Zoe, they're here! There they are! The square is hell, what did I tell you? We'll see everything from here.

Here come the schools! The schools! With their yellow shirts, boys in front, girls at the back. One, two, three, four, five, six, seven, eight, ten, twelve, twelve! They're coming in dozens. (*He jumps up and down, looking out of the window in all directions.*)

And the army! What grandeur! I've never seen such beautiful uniforms! Green, orange, black, turquoise ... There's the gendarmerie. It must be the special police; everyone's on black horses! Their helmets are shining in the sun, it's blinding. And ... right in the front there's one on a white horse. He's holding his sword erect, a big sword with a yellow hilt ... oh! my God, do I see right? That's my friend! ... Yes, it's him. He's not wearing anything on his head, he's got his hair down, that's why I didn't recognize him at first, but now I can see his face, yes, it's him ... But, won't you come and look at him Zoe ... My dear little sister come and see him I beg you. (*Opens the window*) Eh! mate (*He waves.*)

(*Noise fills the room.*)

ZOE: (*shouting*) Shut the window! You know the noise upsets me.

ARIS: [SOUNDS] (*He doesn't pay her attention. Accompanies the drums*) Raparam – rapapami...

ZOE: (*screams covering her ears*) Shut it! Shut it!

(*Sudden silence, while* ARIS *carries on mimicking the drums. Then he stops.* ZOE *moves her hands from her ears and stands questioningly.*)

ZOE: There's no more sound. Have they stopped playing?

ARIS: Yes.

ZOE: What are they doing now?

ZOE: They've stopped all of a sudden.

ARIS: Why?

ARIS: It seems that something's going to happen. They

might unveil the statue I told you about. The people are folding up their umbrellas. Everyone is.

ZOE: There's no more sun?

ARIS: There is. But they seem to want to see better. (*Goes to the right end of the window looking down to the left*) Wait. Something's coming from the side of the church, because everyone is looking in that direction leaning towards it ... Ah, if I could only see, it must be something important because they're pushing each other, they're hurrying to be the one to see first! One has broken away from the barrier ... and another and another ... Ha! They're being pushed back by the boy scouts the smartasses! They're being forced to stand with the others. Yes, it's the boy scouts who are pushing them back inside, for sure. I didn't notice them before (*Happily surprised*) Zoe! They're boy scouts with batons and short trousers ...

ZOE: Boy scouts? Like the ones that follow the Good Friday procession?

ARIS: Yes, like them.

ZOE: Are they making a chain with their hands?

ARIS: Exactly. They're creating a chain to prevent the people from going under the ropes. No one moves again ... They're only watching, watching (*With great excitement*) But what on earth can they see? (*Amazed*) For Goodness sake! Dogs!

ZOE: Dogs?

ARIS: Yes ... what are the dogs doing in a parade? They're coming out and there's no end to them. They must be around a hundred ... They're pulling the dogs into the middle of the square ... They're packing them tightly one next to the other ... I've never seen anything like it! (*To his sister*) Won't you come and see it ... For once drop your knitting and come and see. They're panting with their tongues hanging out (*Mimics a panting dog*) Squashed like that, do you know what they look like? Like a huge colourful ball. The people are still looking at the church. I wonder what else will appear ... wait.

ZOE: What is it? What can you see?

ARIS: I can't see very well ... They're bringing something else (*Not sure*) It looks like a cart. A cart with wooden railings at the side and on the top. Only the end of it is visible though, because it's stopped.

(*Low sound of galloping horses*)

ZOE: What was that?

ARIS: The gendarmerie. They've ridden up to it. Of course, if it is the gendarmerie ... I'm not sure any more. I don't recognize their uniforms.

(*Sound of galloping again*)

ARIS: They've arranged themselves in two sections, as if they're leaving a space for the cart to go through.

(ZOE *stands up and approaches him.*)

ZOE: (*with a timid voice*) Tell me, what's happening now?

ARIS: Wait ... those same people ... they're pushing each other and they're trying to get under the ropes again. Wait a minute – wait a minute. Hey you, mister, with the cap, where do you think you're going? Bark-bark. And you madam, yes you, the one who wants to stand in front of everyone, and you, and you, back to your places at once ... Heh! The boy scouts, they know what they're doing. The cart is starting to move slowly, it's all out now, I can't see very well – the ones on horseback are obstructing my view.

It's not a cart. (*Turns to his sister, amazed*) Zoe! It's a cage, a long narrow cage on wheels and inside there must be animals, because they're jumping up and down, they're holding the rails (*Gets angry*) Oh damn, those men on horses ... they're, they're humans! Zoe! They're carrying humans in the cage!

ZOE: (*climbs up to the window, and looks out as well*) God, how many people have gathered!

ARIS: Look! There! Where I'm pointing at you!

ZOE: The square is full ... The dogs ... show me the dogs ...

ARIS: Have you seen the cage?

ZOE: Where? Where? ... I can't see...

ARIS: Look! It's there, there between the horses...

ZOE: Black horses! Have you counted them?

ARIS: *(angrily)* Look what I'm showing you. What do you see in between the horses?

ZOE: A cage. And there are humans in it.

ARIS: Have you ever seen such a thing?

ZOE: They're naked ... The dogs ... I want to see the dogs.

ARIS: They're old.

ZOE: With long hair.

ARIS: They're shaking the rails.

ZOE: They're acting as if they want to jump out...

ARIS: They're skinny, like skeletons.

ZOE: They're crazy. They're crazy. They're bringing lunatics into the square.

ARIS: Don't ... Don't look any more, don't look!

(ZOE tries to watch, ARIS blocks her.)

ZOE: Let me. I want to see. What is it? What do you see?

ARIS: It's horrible! Haven't you noticed anything?

ZOE: No, tell me quickly, tell me...

ARIS: Those inside, all of them, they're mutilated ... one with no legs, one with no hands ... There's one with no head! My God! I'm right, he's got no head ... And yet, his neck is moving...

ZOE: *(hysterically)* Shut the window quickly, shut it!

ARIS: There are not only old people, there're children in there as well ... There, one is lifting up a child ... Ah!

ZOE: What? What is it?

ARIS: His face is disfigured, burnt...

(The crowd noise gets louder.)

ZOE: *(blocking her eyes)* Shut the window.

(ARIS stands still. Silence. Then a sudden, loud noise)

ZOE: Shut it ... What was that noise? *(Slowly, scared but with morbid curiosity)*

ARIS: The people've broken through the ropes, they are rushing away ... But they're being pushed back again, they're hit. The boy scouts whip them with broken ropes, the others jump off their horses and are hitting them with truncheons. One's got a woman by the hair. He's thrown her down, he's kicking her in the face (*Cries almost*)

ZOE: (*hysterically*) Leave the window, go away quickly ... (*Pause*) Tell me, what do you see?

ARIS: (*smothering a sob in a monotone*) It's quiet again. Everyone's back in place. The middle of the square is empty except for the dogs. And the statue. Even the people in the cage are still. My friend ... him ... the one I was telling you, that's got his hair long, he's going towards the statue. He's clapped his hands. They're looking towards the church again. They're bringing someone. They're pulling him by his hands, because he can't walk on his own, he can't see. (*Starts connecting with the description again and becomes excited*) His head is covered with a cloth, that's why they're leading him. He stumbles at every step he takes, everyone's watching him...

(*A sharp cry*)

ZOE: What is it? What have you seen?

ARIS: I'm scared...

ZOE: (*shaking*) Why are you scared?

ARIS: This man...

ZOE: Go on, go on...

ARIS: He's wearing a blue jacket and underneath a yellow jumper...

ZOE: (*climbs up to the window*) Open the window, I can't see clearly...

ARIS: Wait.

(*They look at each other.*)

ZOE: Is it father?

ARIS: What's he doing out there?

ZOE: He didn't tell us he was coming to the parade.

(*Pause.* ARIS *turns slowly towards the window.*)

ARIS: Look, they're uncovering his face now.

(*Long pause while both look out the window.*)

ZOE: It's not him.

ARIS: It's a stranger! His clothes confused us.

ZOE: Do you know him?

ARIS: No, it's the first time I've seen him.

ZOE: How pale he is. His face is whiter than the cloth that covered it.

ARIS: Look his hands are tied...

ZOE: And his feet.

ARIS: That's why he stumbled like that ... What are they going to do to him?

ZOE: There! They're unveiling the statue! They're uncovering it!

ARIS: It's not a statue.

ZOE: No, it's not a statue ... What is it? Tell me what it is.

ARIS: It's a gallows ... No, it's not a gallows, it's a guillotine ... Like the one they had during the French Revolution, remember in the history book? (*Steps down, grabs a book and starts looking for the picture to check it*)

ZOE: Ari, that guy, the one with the long hair, he's leading him, he's placing him there, there, Ari! They're going to kill him. They're pushing him on to his knees to chop off his head...

(ARIS *hurries to the window.*)

ZOE: Aris, no one's saying anything ... Open the window, call out, do something.

ARIS: (*lost, opens the window. Hubbub*) Hey you ... Hey.

ZOE: They can't hear you.

ARIS: They're leaving ... Leaving the square to hide. Don't you see? They've been chased by the horses. They're firing shot guns. Hey, don't run away! They'll kill him! (*He's almost in tears. Crowd noise and galloping are still audible.*) There's blood on his face.

ZOE: Ari, the dogs! They've let the dogs go and all of them are throwing themselves on him, they're tearing him into pieces.

ARIS: I can't see anything any more, I can't tell what's going on ...

ZOE: Ari, come come away from the window ... That guy with the long hair is watching us.

ARIS: Yes. He's watching us. He saw us ...

ZOE: He's nodding to the others! They'll come here, they will! They're coming ... Ari, they're coming ... No, go away, no ... (*Steps back*)

(ARIS *recovers shortly, looks around him.*)

ZOE: They're coming up the stairs ... They're going to break the door down. (*Rushes to the door, leans against it and screams. She steps back robot-like, with her arms stretched out as if to protect herself.*)

They're coming ... they're coming ... they're coming ...

ARIS: No, no, no.

(*The noise of the crowd is being smothered by the triumphant, marching music, that reaches a peak and then suddenly stops. Blackout*)

The End

Love Thriller

by

George Skourtis

Translated by
Aphroditi Panagiotakou

The Characters

ALEX.
A successful lawyer. He may be disgusted by the legal profession, but for financial and social reasons, he is obliged to 'play the game', even though he feels morally tormented. As a man, a husband and father, he also carries all the psychological burdens of a phallocratic society.

MAGDA.
A fragile personality, with intense emotional, sentimental and existential anxieties.

As a couple they appear tender and loving, but behind this image lies the 'abyss' of their relationship, which they keep pushing 'inwards', but which insists on bursting 'outwards'. This catalytic action and reaction, will bring them gradually to the catharsis, which may be redemption, or catastrophe.

They have a daughter – who does not appear – aged sixteen.

Stage-setting

A tastefully and expensively furnished sitting-room in a semi-detatched house, with an internal staircase, open kitchen, bookcase, desk, dining-table, television and stereo appliances etc.

FIRST PART

First Scene

Music is heard from the stereo – classical or other music, which however should create an atmosphere of supsense. MAGDA *is in the kitchen area, preparing dinner, while at the same time she moves to and from the sitting-room, where she is setting the table with tablecloth, napkins, glasses, plates, wine, candles, flowers etc.*
Two things should be obvious from these ordinary movements. First, that MAGDA *has a bad headache, keeps holding her head and taking aspirins ... The second, that when passing in front of a large mirror, she looks at her body, passing her hands over it, clutching at it, as if she does not feel it, and wishes to do so.*
Following this, the door-bell rings, with a special signal. MAGDA, *lost in her thoughts, is alarmed by the sudden sound. She moves rapidly towards the space leading to the door, but exactly at that point she almost bumps into* ALEX *who is just arriving – dressed in a suit, with his tie loosened, holding a briefcase and files.*
MAGDA *is alarmed once more.*

MAGDA: Oh ... Alex, why do you frighten me like that?

ALEX: (*appears nervous and tired*) Come on Magda, I can't be so frightening!
If I come in using my key, you're frightened because you don't hear me. If I ring in our secret signal, and then open with my key, you're frightened all the same. Fantastic nerves! Did you get them at a bargain price? (*He follows his usual movements on coming home from work.*)

MAGDA: Sorry, darling ... Well, what about yours ... A kiss for me?

(*They kiss gently,* MAGDA *hurries to finish serving dinner.*)

MAGDA: Were you at court?

ALEX: In the office.

MAGDA: Is everything all right?

ALEX: I suppose so, I told you I was in the office.

MAGDA: A client?

ALEX: (*depressed*) A client.

MAGDA: A good one?

ALEX: Like anybody.

MAGDA: Some big dealer or one of those desperate junkies?

ALEX: A penal case. Didn't I tell you I'm not taking any more drug cases?

MAGDA: Well ... if it isn't really necessary ... Are you hungry? Dinner's ready.

ALEX: Necessary! We need too many things! Don't you think darling, that we should stop eating?

MAGDA: Why?

ALEX: So as to stop working.

MAGDA: (*sarcastically*) How would humanity make any progress then?

ALEX: Going where? (*His mobile phone rings, he looks for it, answers.*)

Yes ... Listen, don't you realize that I just came home, to rest, to enjoy the nice dinner my nice little wife prepared and to forget? What? I see! Well, tell him I'll fuck him. Tell him I'll fuck the living daylights ... Nothing, forget it, tomorrow in the office. (*He hangs up and throws it somewhere.*)

These mobile phones are the latest conspiracy of a bloody minority against the majority of jerks, remember my words.

MAGDA: Must you talk like that? Fuck the living daylights!

ALEX: That's what they need. (*Embraces her*) I didn't mean you.

MAGDA: I should hope not!

ALEX: Where is Jenny?

MAGDA: Doing homework with a girlfriend.

ALEX: 'Doing homework with a girlfriend.' Does she never do homework with any boys? Is she to become a lesbian? Are you sure she's telling you the truth?

MAGDA: Come on darling! If she's with a boy you want to know what kind of guy he is, if she's with a girl...

ALEX: We've lost our children these days. When we talk to them we don't know if they're lying or not, what their feelings are. We don't know if in their hearts they love us, or are indifferent, or hate us for something which we ignore completely.

MAGDA: Wasn't it always like that? Weren't we the same with our parents? We smoked secretly, played secretly, cried secretly . . . secretly . . .

ALEX: Yes, go on.

MAGDA: Come on, let's eat. Open the wine. It's a red Burgundy!

ALEX: That's all we need.

(*As he is preparing to sit down at the table, the telephone rings.* MAGDA *is alarmed . . .*)

ALEX: Take it easy! Why don't you lower the damned thing?

MAGDA: (*goes to answer*) I don't hear it if it's too low. Yes . . . hello . . . (*Hangs up*) The lines have gone berserk. Shall I put on some music?

ALEX: No . . . Did the contractor show up today? No, don't tell me, I know.

MAGDA: Unfortunately.

ALEX: Things have reached the point of no return, I'm telling you. There's nothing we can do. Whoever resists becomes a laughing stock. Who do you think you are, you jerk? they say. Do you think we're jerks, simply because we go along with the game?

(*They have already started eating.*)

ALEX: That country-house is draining all our resources. Today I insured it against fire.

MAGDA: Do you think that might be their next target? Oh, no!

ALEX: Why not? We could spend the insurance money on drink, pot, coke . . . you only live once!

MAGDA: What would happen to our little Jen?

ALEX: Lovely dinner! Congratulations, my dear.

MAGDA: Congratulations to you too, my dear provider. Do you really like it?

ALEX: Have you never heard the saying that 'he married her

because she made perfect moussakas'?

MAGDA: Only that?

ALEX: That's about somebody else, you do everything well. Let's say you do.

MAGDA: (*stops eating*) What is that supposed to mean?

ALEX: Nothing. At least we have good Burgundy wine.

MAGDA: (*stops his glass in mid-air*) People say cheers.

(*They clink glasses.*)

MAGDA: Is something wrong?

ALEX: I'm tense, what else?

MAGDA: Why, what happened?

ALEX: That client today ... forget it, I'll tell you later. How is Jen?

MAGDA: She's fine, our lovely child. Only today ... they found syringes at her school.

ALEX: (*hits his hand on the table and then rises*) Don't tell me, shit! The bloody bastards!

MAGDA: (*rises too*) I'm sorry, darling, sorry. I shouldn't have told you.

ALEX: Of course you should have! Do you know this girlfriend of hers?

MAGDA: You know her too. She was at her birthday party. That little blonde.

ALEX: The one with cropped hair?

MAGDA: Don't make a fuss! They're just kids. Sometimes they wear it long, then short, blonde, red, yellow...

ALEX: Do you know her father?

MAGDA: An excellent person. He's really fond of Jen.

ALEX: What do you mean he's fond of her? Does he cuddle her, touch her in a fatherly way, fondle her little arms and legs?

MAGDA: What are you talking about? Our own child?

ALEX: That's what I mean, our own child! Search all her drawers and the pockets of all her clothes.

MAGDA: I can't do that to my own child. You do it.

ALEX: You're the mother.

MAGDA: And you're the father.

ALEX: You might find pot, or pills.

MAGDA: Aren't you overdoing it? We should know our own child.

ALEX: That's what people think, that they don't have to worry, and then all of a sudden you find satanists, drug addicts and call girls everywhere.

MAGDA: Come on now darling, take it easy. Let's have dinner.

ALEX: I don't ever want to eat again. Pour me a drink. (*His mobile rings.*) Oh, bugger off.

(*He finds it, answers, while* MAGDA *pours him a drink.*)

ALEX: Yes ... speaking ... hello ... not yet ... I'll study the legal deed, and tomorrow, as we agreed, I'll give you an answer ... certainly ... yes, yes, I understand ... I have a session in court at twelve ... yes ... good bye ... (*Hangs up*)

MAGDA: (*gives him the drink*) What is the case about?

ALEX: (*lights a cigarette*) Tell me, what did you do today?

MAGDA: (*starts clearing the table, and putting things in the kitchen*)

Nothing. I just called the flower-arrangers, and asked for information.

ALEX: What flower-arrangers?

MAGDA: Didn't I tell you I wanted to learn flower-arranging?

ALEX: I don't remember.

MAGDA: I'm not surprised.

ALEX: What about?

MAGDA: Never mind. It will be fun. You learn how to make all kinds of decorations with bouquets, branches and leaves.

ALEX: How many hours will you be away? Where will you leave Jenny?

MAGDA: Come on now, she's sixteen, she can be left alone. Anyway I'm not going. That's what I wanted to tell you. While I was thinking about making bouquets, I had a fantastic idea.

ALEX: (*sarcastically*) To learn how to pour steel.

MAGDA: (*ignores him*) I'll write a novel.

ALEX: ZZZZZZboom. You abandoned literature for poetry, then it was art history, and now that's over too...

MAGDA: (*stares at him with a stubborn expression*) I won't abandon this until I've finished.

ALEX: Half the population are writers, which would be all right if the other half were readers.

MAGDA: I'm a reader, and I'll write it too. I love the idea. It's the first time something has really got hold of me. I've been thinking about it all day. While listening to music, or reading or cooking I couldn't think of anything else.

What are your plans for the evening, are you going out with some friend?

ALEX: Why all this hurry, why do you have to know so early?

MAGDA: If you're not going out, as soon as Jen goes to bed, it would be nice to sit here together, and get some really good ideas for my novel.

ALEX: With whom would I go out anyway? There's nobody left.

MAGDA: What about that colleague you went out with the other day?

ALEX: Oh, that guy! A bag of shit!

MAGDA: Why, what happened?

ALEX: Nothing. Nothing good. Any news from the bank?

MAGDA: None at all.

ALEX: They're waiting. As soon as it's finished, they'll grab it. This mortgage is going to be a nightmare. Oh, and no more credit cards. I can hardly breathe.

Easy money, they say. All for free, they say. That's the nightmare.

MAGDA: Aren't you getting a down-payment from your client, so that we can give the contractor something?

ALEX: I don't know if I'm taking the case. I smell trouble.

MAGDA: What do you mean?

ALEX: Do you have the blonde girl's phone number?

MAGDA: Of course I do.

ALEX: Why don't you call, and see if Jenny's there?

MAGDA: Where else would she be?

ALEX: Isn't it better if you call?

MAGDA: I'll call darling, I'll call, just a minute.

(She looks for her agenda, and goes to the phone, while ALEX opens his file...)

MAGDA: *(speaks on the phone)* Yes, hello, I'm Jenny's mother, how are you? Fine, fine ... is Jen there? ... Yes poor kids, they work so hard ... no, nothing, I just called to say hello, her father wanted to ask her if they were going to the theatre, you know father – daughter, like love-birds ... thank you so much ... *(To ALEX)* Hurry!

ALEX: *(hurries to pick up the receiver)* Yes, how's my baby? ... Fine ... I said fine ... Are we going to the theatre? On Saturday? Great ... What are they playing? Oh no, are you taking me to see a Greek play? By whom? Oh, I dig him ... All right baby ... Anything you say, your highness, I kiss your hand, ciao.

(He hangs up ... in a better mood, embraces MAGDA and leads her to the couch, kissing her in a sexy way. MAGDA however, seems to draw back ... ALEX pushes her onto the couch, tickling her, but finally MAGDA manages to get up.)

MAGDA: Now it's my turn for a glass of whiskey.

ALEX: *(sits up on the couch, appearing offended)* Great...

MAGDA: Would you like another? It's on me. Then I'll tell you about the wonderful inspiration I had. I can't wait until tonight.

ALEX: Is it a thriller?

MAGDA: Don't be a spoilsport.

ALEX: Allow me to say I know something about Magda's mind.

MAGDA: It's not just any thriller. It's THE thriller!

ALEX: Would you like some special music, suspence and the like?

MAGDA: Why not, put something on.

(ALEX goes to put the music on while MAGDA fixes the drinks and takes an aspirin as well...
They approach the couch, light cigarettes...)

ALEX: Ready.

MAGDA: (*with a storytelling expression*) So ... there is a woman...

ALEX: Holding a glass of whiskey.

MAGDA: Listen, listen ... She has this recurring dream ... A man ... Like a black threatening shadow ... She can't tell ... But this man is dangerous, as if ... he wants something evil ... Listen to what happens next! One day this woman – not in her dream any more – meets a man on the street, and immediately her mind and her soul remember the man she dreamt of, her nightmare.

She's sure it's him, and he's a total stranger.

(*End of the story*)

That's all for now. I thought it all up today. You can say it's a coincidence, or that I'm exaggerating, but my headache was cured. It started again, of course, later, but ... What do you think?

ALEX: (*already his mood appears worse*) Go on.

MAGDA: Oh, I don't know, this is where I need some real inspired thinking.

I'll find it. I'm sure. I've got this feeling deep inside, that I must write this novel. It will be a release for me!

ALEX: (*tensely*) From what? (*He turns off the music.*)

MAGDA: From the burdens of my soul and my body (*Tenderly*) Then you'll see the real Magda again.

ALEX: I hope so ... I assure you I'll do my utmost to make it a best-seller. I'll send my secretary to buy up all the copies.

MAGDA: I don't care if it's published. I only want to write it. Would you like an aspirin?

ALEX: Have you finished the box again?

MAGDA: Not exactly ... I only had two or three.

ALEX: You know you shouldn't. It's one or none.

MAGDA: One is none.

(*The home telephone rings.* MAGDA *jumps to answer and* ALEX *throws her a glance, surprised about her anxiety, then goes to the phone.*)

ALEX: Yes, hello ... (*Hangs up*) I wonder, when the phone rings, is it somebody or not?

MAGDA: (*as a pun*) Well, it might be nobody.

(*The phone rings again.*)

MAGDA: I'll get it ... (*Answers*) Hello ... yes ... how are you? ...

(ALEX *motions that he is not there.*)

MAGDA: No, Alex isn't here, can I give him a message? Of course ... all the best, good bye. (*Hangs up*) It was the friend you went out with the other day. He called to ...

ALEX: The bastard!

MAGDA: There's something wrong with you today. Why don't you lie down for a while?

ALEX: Why should I lie down? If you lie down and can't sleep you go crazy.

Then they say: A hundred thousand.

MAGDA: Who?

ALEX: That client who came over today. Can you believe the bastard?

MAGDA: Is he that rich?

ALEX: I'm telling you he's a bastard, how could he be poor?

MAGDA: So?

ALEX: What do you mean so? ... (*Gets tense*) Six for the bank, twelve for the contractor, fifteen for the builders, seven and a half for the floors, nine for the doors, six for the electrician, nine for the alarm-system, the stars for the architect, the sun and the moon for the engineer and the plumber, three for commissions ... There, we're already over the budget. Not even rape could save us! (*Now that he's said it ... he waits for* MAGDA*'s reaction.*)

MAGDA: (*naturally doesn't understand*) Rape? What rape?

ALEX: Rape. A rape case. The client I was telling you about ...

MAGDA: Oh ... did the girl herself come or ...

ALEX: The father ... of the rapist.

MAGDA: I don't understand.

ALEX: An upper-class young man raped a girl, and his father promised me a hundred thousand if he gets away

with it. It happened two years ago, he avoided custody
owing to his father's contacts, but he didn't get away with
the trial. Both sides pushed things to extremes.

MAGDA: Did he rape her?

ALEX: What do you think?

MAGDA: Are you taking on the case?

ALEX: I don't know.

MAGDA: Good heavens, what we women have to put up
with. You make our lives a nightmare.

ALEX: (*sarcastically and agressively*) Does that include me?

MAGDA: I'm talking about male justice darling. Come on,
give me a kiss!

(*They kiss gently.*)

MAGDA: Will you help me to write the novel?

ALEX: What do I know about the subject?

MAGDA: You can be my legal adviser.

ALEX: I'm a lawyer, and I only enjoy reading about lawyers.
Write about me, and I'll help you.

MAGDA: I'll find a place for you as well. Shall we go inside,
and I'll give you a relaxing massage?

ALEX: If you massage me, you turn me on. But you're never
in the mood. I don't want a massage, I want you. I can't
even remember when the last time was you wanted me!

MAGDA: Come on, sweetheart. Everything will be all right,
you'll see. These headaches drive me crazy, my body feels
dead.
Anyway I know you sow your wild oats ... no, no, don't
tell me anything, I don't mind, we're not only that.

ALEX: We're that too.

MAGDA: Yes, but not only.

ALEX: (*losing his patience*) That, dammit, that!

MAGDA: (*gives up*) All right ... if you say so.

(*Minutes pass ... they light cigarettes.*)

MAGDA: What are you thinking about?

ALEX: Jenny...

MAGDA: Yes?

ALEX: Do you know ... if she's made love?

MAGDA: She'd probably tell you first.

ALEX: She would?

MAGDA: Well, it's about time, isn't it?

ALEX: What do you mean?

MAGDA: What do you think, darling? My first time was at fifteen.

ALEX: (*sarcastically*) How the hell was it?

MAGDA: Hell! (*An indirect innuendo*) Until you came along and showed me heaven.

ALEX: Now what's that supposed to mean?

MAGDA: My head darling. I must have an aspirin. (*She goes to the kitchen, takes an aspirin and water, turns towards* ALEX, *watches him watching her, and slowly washes down the aspirin.*)

(*Darkness falls slowly, while they keep looking at each other...*)

Second Scene

It's evening ... The sitting-room is lit by a table-lamp and the staircase is dimly lit ... MAGDA *comes home, with coat, handbag etc. She looks around to see if anyone's there, then looks upstairs from the banister ... She speaks in a whisper.*

MAGDA: Jenny, are you asleep, baby? Can you hear me? Sleep well, my sweetheart ... You'll take care, won't you? Even in your dreams, take care.
A thousand kisses.

(*Takes off her shoes – but not her coat – pours herself a drink and moves forwards slowly, absorbed in her thoughts ... Takes her cigarettes out of her handbag, puts one in her mouth and gets ready to light it.*
The door is heard opening, and immediately she lets the cigarette fall onto the floor, as she hurriedly puts the glass down, gathers up her shoes and goes up the stairs.
In two minutes ALEX *enters ... Listens around too ... Pours*

himself a drink, picks up MAGDA's *cigarette from the floor, looks at it, puts it into mouth and lights it. He inhales twice, thinking, then puts it out and moves towards the staircase...*)

(*Darkness*)

Third Scene

Next day ... Music is heard, Callas singing 'Vissi d'arte' by Puccini. MAGDA *is in the kitchen ... Interrupting her work, she comes into the sitting-room, sits on the couch, picks up a note-book and writes something down.*

Thinks ... Writes some more ... Gets up, and goes to the kitchen, stares at her body in the mirror, in the same way as the first scene – goes back to the kitchen, busies herself with the food she is preparing ... returns to the sitting-room and devotes herself completely to thinking and taking notes.

The door is heard closing, but MAGDA *does not interrupt her activity. As soon as* ALEX *enters and speaks to her, she is alarmed.*

ALEX: How are things?

MAGDA: Oh ... sorry darling, I was absorbed in my thriller. You'll never guess what I came up with.

ALEX: I came up with something too.

MAGDA: Really? Tell me.

ALEX: Wait a moment, I just got in.

MAGDA: Where's my kiss? You've been here for ages and haven't kissed me yet.

ALEX: (*kisses her*) My head's all in a turmoil. She may be a prima donna all right, but please turn it off (*He means the music.*)

MAGDA: I lived for art and love, she says!

ALEX: For the art of lying and fucking? Are there any aspirins left?

MAGDA: Heaps ... (*She goes to bring him one.*) But you don't suffer from headaches. (*Turns off the music.*)

ALEX: Yes, have you forgotten ... that time you came to

court and beat a hasty retreat?

MAGDA: God forbid! I'd go crazy in there. Come on, go and wash off the day's grime, and come over here! Today I've prepared your favourite dish.

I hope your secretary hasn't told you already.

ALEX: She forgets my appointments in court, do you think she remembers your stuffed tomatoes?

MAGDA: She told you! (*Gives him an aspirin and water.*)

ALEX: Silly girl, the TV cameramen are fighting in the street, for an on-the-spot report about your tomatoes red as blood. The whole neighbourhood smells fantastic. (*Swallows the aspirin*)

MAGDA: So I got them right!

ALEX: Yes, but don't serve them yet. Pour me a drink first, my mouth's dry.

(*He moves towards the inner rooms, bathroom etc.* MAGDA *prepares his drink.* ALEX *can be heard speaking.*)

ALEX: Did Jenny call?

MAGDA: Twice. She's having a great time. Sends her love. (*Observes her body in the mirror, goes into the kitchen and nibbles something . . .*)

(ALEX *comes in.*)

ALEX: I'm dying for that drink, where is it?

MAGDA: Over there, next to your briefcase.

ALEX: Great . . . Guess what!

MAGDA: A present? I love it when you bring me presents!

ALEX: (*takes a small parcel out of the briefcase*) Pills! Latest fashion, strictly for sleeping.

MAGDA: Wonderful darling, at last I'll get some sleep. Where did you get them?

ALEX: That friend of mine, the psychiatrist gave them to me. Don't take them all together . . . Cheers. (*Sips his drink*)

MAGDA: Cheers, cheerio . . . So, what were you going to tell me?

ALEX: Well . . . I found a publisher for you. But he said he wants you to write something different, something romantic, not a thriller and that kind of thing.

All bestsellers are rubbish, but if that's what people want, what can we do?

MAGDA: (*is offended*) I care about what I want, not other people.

ALEX: I'm telling you for your own peace of mind.

MAGDA: My peace of mind is in here, in my head. Will you help me to write it? Say you will.

ALEX: You'll drive me nuts. I've got my own problems.

MAGDA: . . . Your problems are mine too, but what about mine? Must I face them alone? For example, listen – inspired by your client's case, I thought I'd make the man want to rape her . . . I mean in her dreams . . . What happens when she meets him on the street though? Does she introduce herself? Hello, how are you, I'm the one dreaming of you trying to rape her?

ALEX: Sounds improbable, doesn't it?

MAGDA: What does he do? How would you react?

ALEX: I'd take her to the psychiatrist, that's what I'd do.

MAGDA: Come on, tell me!

ALEX: What can I say baby? (*He wants a cigarette, but his packet is empty.*) There goes another packet. There's one in my jacket, could you please bring it to me?

(MAGDA *goes, while* ALEX *opens his file.*)

MAGDA: Maybe she could follow him? To see where and how he lives, become his shadow?

ALEX: Why don't you make her rape him? That would be fun.

MAGDA: (*lights his cigarette, inhales once, and gives it to him*) Why not? I wish women could rape too. That would teach you a lesson. From a legal and penal view-point, what is the exact definition of rape?

ALEX: (*in an official legal tone*) The penetration of the penis, the union of sexual organs, in an extramarital relationship, – in marriage too, now – under life-threatening conditions, or physical violence, impossible to resist by the person under threat.

MAGDA: Only in that case?

ALEX: In what other?

MAGDA: Isn't rape of the soul acknowledged by the law?

ALEX: Naturally. Psychological violence also exists. Tell me, how many times has she dreamt of him?

MAGDA: I don't know ... Once, twice ... twenty times.

ALEX: Who is he, and why does she dream of him? You need that to make the story.

MAGDA: I just wrote that down! (*Shows him her notebook*) There it is, underlined too. Who and why? ... I don't know yet, I'll find the answer. Guess what else I've been thinking. I'll make her shiver like jelly when she meets him, want to run away, but she can't, she's petrified.

ALEX: (*testing her*) But you said before, that in her dream she only discerns a black shadow, how can she recognize someone particular she meets by chance?

MAGDA: I don't know ... just like that ... I'm talking about dream-like feelings, you know I get carried away by that kind of thing.

ALEX: Sounds a tangle.

MAGDA: Well darling, what kind of thriller would it be, otherwise?

ALEX: The human soul is unfathomable. So is Magda's. Just look at what your poor sore head made up!

MAGDA: Maybe I got the idea the other evening, when somebody followed me.

ALEX: (*losing his patience*) That's enough now! Really Magda, you've reached the limit, take care! We'll both end up in the madhouse! You'd stopped raving and tossing in your sleep, do you remember ... you've started again lately. Take it easy!

MAGDA: What do I rave about in my sleep?

ALEX: Nothing. You moan.

MAGDA: Why didn't you tell me?

ALEX: What could I tell you? You tell me!

MAGDA: (*changes the subject, but maintains the same mood*) The contractor called.

ALEX: (*lights a cigarette, relaxes a bit*) High time too! Money

I suppose, eh?

MAGDA: I told him to get on, and he'd get his money, was that right?

ALEX: It sure was ... (*Opens a file*)

MAGDA: I was thinking about my parents' house too...

ALEX: So?

MAGDA: We haven't been for ages. I wonder how it is.

ALEX: It will be fine ... Old houses die hard.

MAGDA: It's curious. Even though the house was my mother's property, we always mentioned it as father's. Have you ever heard anyone say I'm going to my motherland?

ALEX: No. (*Shows her something he takes out from the file*) Do you know these mugs?

MAGDA: Are they politicians?

ALEX: Well ... I told you they're mugs – could they be cherubs?

MAGDA: Who are they?

ALEX: The litigants.

(*The phone rings.*)

MAGDA: Just a minute darling ... (*Answers*) Hello ... Yes sweetheart! Are you having a good time? Yes, yes, he's here ... (*To* ALEX) It's Jen.

ALEX: (*goes to the phone*) Hello, baby ... is the excursion fun? Walks?
Fine ... Don't forget to take snapshots ... This evening? I'll come and pick you up ... lots of love (*Hangs up*)

MAGDA: When are they coming back?

ALEX: (*slightly displeased*) This evening.

MAGDA: What's wrong now? Aren't you happy you spoke to her?

ALEX: Come on now, I would be happy, I would dance from joy, but this damned thing won't let me (*Indicates his head*) Just like yours.

MAGDA: Come on now, what bothered you?

ALEX: Nothing now, but the other day that friend I went out with, after drinks we went to his office, which he uses as a love-nest too, with a bed, a video ... and what does

he show me? A hard-core movie! 'School excursion'!
With teenaged girls, screwing with the teachers, learning
the secrets of sex.
That's a real thriller! So, you were telling me about
somebody following you.
What then?

MAGDA: The usual. Being women, we always have somebody behind us.

ALEX: Is that why you always get on?

MAGDA: Very funny, a real sense of humour!

ALEX: Are you telling me what happened?

MAGDA: Nothing. I just felt somebody behind me in the dark.

ALEX: Why were you walking in the dark?

MAGDA: It was a lovely evening and I felt like walking, that's
all. What else could I do, sprint from one streetlight to the
other?

ALEX: (*pours another drink*) Go on.

MAGDA: Well, I was scared. But I liked it.

ALEX: What?

MAGDA: My fear. Even though I was afraid, I was happy to
feel the fear.

ALEX: (*doesn't understand*) I see . . .

MAGDA: Even if he hadn't left, I would have walked on, to
feel him behind me, to feel the fear . . .

ALEX: Now I need a dozen aspirins.

MAGDA: Kidding me, eh? . . . The same thing happened last
night.

ALEX: What?

MAGDA: Somebody followed me again.

ALEX: The same one?

MAGDA: How should I know? I don't turn round to look.
Maybe my imagination . . .

ALEX: I must say, you imagine weird things these days.

MAGDA: Shall I put some music on? (*Goes to put on the music*)
You haven't told me, are you assuming that 'dirty case'?

ALEX: Why do you say 'dirty case'? All cases are the same.
Thieves, frauds, killers, rapists, whores, impostors, scum,
beggars, schemers in high places, pimps, drug addicts,

maniacs ... They are my everyday buddies.

Something more. They are our daily bread. Money passes from their hands to mine, then to yours ... Turn that music off!

MAGDA: Is your rapist's defence easy? (*She turns the music off.*)

ALEX: I can only tell you what Balzac once said – 'It's impossible to thread a moving needle'. Find the thread, and the eye of the needle, and maybe you will understand the consequences of a charge for rape.

MAGDA: That's no news! Women are always the bloody temptation, men are men, women are whores! The rapist's innocence will be the poor girl's official certificate of prostitution. How are you going to prove he's innocent?

ALEX: That's my job. Everything is possible. My rival is a famous defence criminal lawyer. If I win, I'll become a star.

MAGDA: Of rapists?

ALEX: Wake up! The parents of the litigants are political rivals in the same election area. Now guess how and why they ended up in court.

MAGDA: Stop please! I can't bear any more! (*Goes to get a drink of water*)

ALEX: More aspirin?

MAGDA: If we're not having the stuffed tomatoes, lets have the aspirins.

(MAGDA *drinks her glass of water ... They stay where they are, at a distance, absorbed in their separate thoughts...*)

ALEX: What are you thinking about?

MAGDA: Nothing.

ALEX: (*tells her a story*) He asks her. 'What are you thinking?' 'Nothing,' she answers. 'I never think, thoughts tire me. But when I think, I think of nothing'.

MAGDA: (*asking herself*) Could the headaches be caused by the dreams?

ALEX: What dreams?

MAGDA: They say that if you have bad dreams which you can't remember, you can go crazy?

ALEX: What do you dream about?

MAGDA: If only I could remember.

(ALEX *sits on the couch.* MAGDA *approaches slowly, sits on the carpet in front of him, and puts her head on his knees ... She takes his hand and hits her head with it.*)

MAGDA: Press it! ... Tightly!...

(ALEX *caresses her with massaging movements.*)

MAGDA: Do you love me?

ALEX: (*in a sarcastic, disappointed tone*) You love me, I love you, you love me, I love you, you love me, I love you ... if you repeat it a hundred times, you'll see it doesn't mean anything.

MAGDA: I know. As if my heart didn't know you loved me!

ALEX: Come now, darling.

MAGDA: (*jumps up in alarm*) Please say my name! Hurry, say it!

ALEX: (*as if he's saying 'now what's wrong?'*) Magda...

MAGDA: Oh, thank you! I didn't tell you what happened some time ago, so as not to make you worry. It was terrifying! I was on the bus, and all of a sudden I couldn't remember my name any more! 'Who am I?' I kept thinking, 'what's my name?' I couldn't remember, I was really upset, the person next to me, the people standing, watched me searching like crazy in my handbag for my identity card, suddenly I remembered I had lost it, and then I panicked! I jumped up, pressed all the buttons to make the driver stop, got down in a frenzy, and rushed to a phone-booth. My mother was really taken aback. 'Say my name quickly,' I asked her ... As soon as I heard it I came back to myself.

ALEX: (*to calm her and make her happy*) Would you like to go out tonight?

MAGDA: Really? The two of us, like old times? Oh, that would be lovely!

Where are you taking me?

ALEX: Any place you like best.

MAGDA: Great, wonderful! As soon as Jen comes back, we

eat our stuffed tomatoes, wish her sweet dreams and go
out, right?

ALEX: All right.

MAGDA: (*puts her head on his knees again*) You'll see, my
headache will go away too. If only I could find out all
about this woman, and get it written.

(ALEX *makes an irritated gesture in the air with his hands.*
MAGDA *can't see him.*)

MAGDA: You know, lately I keep thinking of the room I
slept in when I was small, in my parents' home. Mice kept
running about, all over the rotten ceiling. Bzzzz fssss.
They drove me crazy! I had that long stick – have I told
you before?

ALEX: Yes, I remember. (*Can't bear listening to her*)

MAGDA: I kept banging the ceiling, bang, bang, to frighten
them, so they would be silent, or go away somewhere,
anywhere.

ALEX: Relax.

MAGDA: That's what I'm saying. Like mice inside my head.
(*Hits her head with his hand*) Hit it, hit it!

ALEX: (*lets out a sudden cry of anguish, as if he was inside a
tunnel*) Aaaaaaaaaaaaaaa!...

(*Darkness cuts him off.*)

Fourth Scene

The same afternoon. MAGDA *is in the sitting-room. She is writing
and thinking, soft music is heard in the background ... The phone
rings, and she runs to answer before it rings too many times.*

MAGDA: Hello ... Who's speaking? ... What do you want?
You should be ashamed of yourself!

(*Apparently, whoever it was, has hung up ... She remains
holding the receiver, then replaces it ... Appears upset. Goes
towards the hall and listens in the direction of the other rooms,*

then lowers the music ... Goes to the fridge, takes a bottle of water and drinks ... The phone rings again, she rushes to answer, choking on the water.)

MAGDA: Yes ... yes ... hello. (*She hangs up ... puts the bottle down, comes back to the sitting-room, lights a cigarette, picks up her note-book and pen, tries to think, but can't concentrate, looks in the direction of the phone.*)

ALEX: (*appears from inside, wearing his dressing-gown*) What's going on?

MAGDA: Did I wake you?

ALEX: No hope of sleeping! I was reading the legal report and newspaper cuttings.

MAGDA: Are you hungry? Would you like a bite of stuffed tomatoes? (*Turns the music off*)

ALEX: At supper with Jen. Who was it on the phone?

MAGDA: (*doesn't want to tell him*) Nobody ... wrong number.

ALEX: Will you make me a special coffee, with your magical touch?

MAGDA: Sure, right away.

(MAGDA *goes towards the kitchen,* ALEX *to the sitting-room, they meet, kiss gently,* ALEX *goes to the sitting-room to light a cigarette.*)

MAGDA: Is the legal report interesting? I mean is it helpful for the defence?

ALEX: The game of rape – figuratively of course – is based on the difference and the tension between the rapist's aggressive tendency, and the victim's terror. If the rapist's agressive and extremely threatening 'I want' is not proven simultaneously to the defenceless victim's 'I don't want', rape cannot be established. As always, darling. Lust, and Violence are the two primary driving forces in the history of mankind. (*Tastes the coffee*)

MAGDA: Is it the way you like it?

ALEX: Even better, thank you.

MAGDA: What does your client assert?

ALEX: That she attacked him. He says she was drunk, and grabbed his genitals, so that he almost lost control of the car and risked a serious accident.

MAGDA: Did the forensic surgeon establish rape?

ALEX: Rape is one of the crimes which cannot be established with absolute certainty. Only the victim's testimony
can prove it – if of course proved true, and the rest of the
evidence is also in favour. For example, in a murder case,
the victim's dead body is a witness of the murderer. In
rape, the victim's living corpse is the witness of its soul's
murderer.

MAGDA: That's really good, I must write it down. (*Takes
notes while she talks*) Will you promise me something?

ALEX: Like what?

MAGDA: Whatever happens, don't humiliate that poor girl.
Grant justice.

ALEX: Justice is not my job.

MAGDA: But how . . .

ALEX: (*interrupts her angrily*) My job is the law. According to
the law, I must defend the rights of the accused. Whether
he is a rapist, a maniac killer, or an incestuous person.
That's what the law, and my vow to the law decrees!

MAGDA: Dont' shout please!

ALEX: Sorry . . . I want you to realize that by protecting my
client's civil rights, I'm protecting the law, and that means
you, our child, society as a whole, and the future of this
world.

MAGDA: I know, sweetheart, I know.

ALEX: Don't tell Jenny anything yet . . . I don't know, I'll see.

MAGDA: As you like. You tell her.

ALEX: I said: I'll see how, and when I will!

(*The phone rings.*)

MAGDA: (*doesn't want to answer it*) Let it ring . . . it's
probably a wrong number.

ALEX: What if Jenny's back?

MAGDA: All right, all right (*Answers*) Hello . . . Who's
speaking? You've got the wrong number . . . (*Hangs up
. . . but seems upset*) What was I saying?
The Social Welfare Organization, they said. They drive us

crazy. From my experience, that is life, a rapist never
believes he is raping, he isn't fully aware that he's killing a
woman's body and soul, because a primordial voice from
his innermost being is saying 'Give it to her, that's what
she wants'.

ALEX: Psychiatric case histories, mention many examples of
women, who actually desired rape.

MAGDA: I bet! With all your blather and talk, next thing you'll
be saying we implore you. By your hand I gladly perish!

ALEX: (*doesn't like the discussion and her irritation*) I'm going
to lie down.

MAGDA: Sweet dreams.

ALEX: (*hesitates*) Was that sarcastic?

MAGDA: Not at all, darling, why should it be sarcastic? You
go and get some rest, while I get on with my thriller. Oh, I
must tell you an idea Jen had.

ALEX: Can you tell me later?

MAGDA: I'll tell you now, then you tell me, and while you're
having your nap, I'll think of the rest.

ALEX: (*agreeably*) Come on, lets hear it then.

MAGDA: Do you remember I told you I had forgotten my
name?

ALEX: How could I ever forget?

MAGDA: Well, Jen had this idea, that the woman suffers
from amnesia and that's why she can't remember who the
man is, and why she has nightmares about him.

ALEX: Amnesia?

MAGDA: You can say repression. The so-called traumatic
memories.

ALEX: What about the shock experience?

MAGDA: I'll find something . . . physical . . . psychological . . .

ALEX: Why do you keep tormenting yourself, darling!

MAGDA: I like the idea, it's good! Terrorized by something!
Jen is really smart.

ALEX: Terrorized by something? By what?

MAGDA: I'll find it, I will. Come on now, go and lie down,
because we're going out tonight, aren't we?

ALEX: Did you search her things? Did you find anything?

MAGDA: I can't do that, I told you.

ALEX: Guess what else the legal report mentions! The victim asserts that she was raped, but confesses that at the last minute she herself gave him a condom.

Have you ever heard anything like it?

MAGDA: Come on, they get that stuff even at school these days.

ALEX: Information is one thing, going around with their pockets full of condoms, is another question. Who will believe she was raped?

MAGDA: Did he threaten her? Did he give her drugs?

ALEX: That's what she says. That he gave her hash. Offering drugs to a person under age sends you directly to trial by jury. In any case, even a rapist is considered innocent until otherwise proven.

MAGDA: Oh my God, you guys will drive us completely crazy!

ALEX: Which guys do you mean?

MAGDA: Men of course, who else? Do you know the difference in numbers between male and female prison occupants?

ALEX: I should know. Two thirds are men.

MAGDA: Whilst in lunatic asylums, two thirds are women. The reason is the anatomical difference in our sexual organs. Yours are external, that's why you express your agressiveness and end up in prison, while we keep everything inside, and end up in the madhouse.

ALEX: (*sarcastically*) *Cosmopolitan* page 21?

MAGDA: Woman, page of the soul.

(*The phone rings.*)

MAGDA: Don't answer!

ALEX: (*is nearby, and picks it up*) Yes ... baby, you've arrived? Good ...

Why shouldn't I come? With a classmate's brother? Hadn't we agreed about that? ... I'm not tired ... I'm coming. I'm coming! (*Hangs up and goes inside hurriedly, to get dressed*)

MAGDA: What's going on?

ALEX: They arrived earlier ... (*Comes out from the inside rooms*)

(MAGDA *remains standing, thinking sadly...*)

(*Darkness*)

Fifth Scene

They return from their evening out ... drunk, tired and tense.
There is an undercurrent of suspense, because now they have drunk, they will express more about their 'abyss' ... As soon as they enter, they immediately make the usual movements on coming home, take off their clothes etc.
ALEX *enters, holding a glass, has a last sip.*

ALEX: One for the road! (*Pours a fresh drink*)

MAGDA: Sshhh, be quiet or you'll wake Jen!

ALEX: How do you know she's asleep?

MAGDA: At this hour! She must be exhausted after the excursion!

ALEX: Kids don't get tired on excursions, they fly like birds.

MAGDA: (*giving the words her own meaning*) Yes ... our Jen flew today too.

ALEX: What do you mean?

MAGDA: Like you said, she flew.

ALEX: Oh ... I'll have another drink, what about you?

MAGDA: No way! I have to piss, I can't wait any longer!

ALEX: (*shows her the empty glass*) Here. It's the same colour. I'll put some ice, too.

MAGDA: Are you still thinking of the woman in the bar, honey? (*Runs inside*)

ALEX: (*prepares the drink*) Nice little whore though, wasn't she?

MAGDA: (*from inside*) Sshhh!

(ALEX *takes the drink, has a sip, goes to the bottom of the staircase, hurriedly takes off his shoes, goes up two steps,*

listens, comes down drinking. We hear the toilet running . . .
MAGDA *comes in, goes to get a glass of water and a pill.*)

ALEX: What are you drinking?

MAGDA: Water . . .

ALEX: Are you in your right mind? You've been drinking! A sleeping pill with alcohol! (*Tries to stop her*)

MAGDA: (*evades his grasp*) Leave me alone! Come on. I know what I'm doing. It's a fanstastic combination! Leaves you unconscious! Why should I wake up every hour?

ALEX: All right . . . Next thing you'll be hearing rats in your head, not just mice. (*Collapses onto the couch*) Our baby is asleep.

MAGDA: Didn't I tell you so? She's asleep and dreaming.

ALEX: Who knows what she dreams about. You have no idea how many times I've wondered. Who knows what she dreams about.

MAGDA: The sea, the sea, the sea! That's what she told me. She always dreams of the sea. What happy dreams she has!

ALEX: What sea? What kind of sea? What does she do, swim?

MAGDA: What else?

ALEX: According to a certain theory, do you know what the sea means? Sexual fantasies!

MAGDA: According to a certain theory, that's fine. When I dream of the sea, I'm always drowning. I sink to the bottom. Plonk, splash. Oh, I feel rested now. My ankles were hurting, my hips, my back! I don't see why you like standing at the bar so much.

ALEX: Well, it has it's own magic darling! If you have the right company!

MAGDA: Well, wasn't the woman in the bar nice?

ALEX: Sure.

MAGDA: Have you ever dreamt of her in the sea?

ALEX: It's the first time I've see her.

MAGDA: Well, maybe tomorrow . . . or tonight . . .

ALEX: What are you trying to say? Just because I said I liked her?

MAGDA: Because you called her a little whore.

ALEX: Come on, I didn't call her a harlot!

MAGDA: I don't have anything against the woman, she seems a nice person, but she was like a wild animal inside a cage, whom other wild animals stare at, and we know very well what they're thinking. I looked at her too, and I thought it might be nice to go out together some time.

ALEX: Whatever for? (*Goes to get another drink*)

MAGDA: We could go out, have a drink and chat. Do you never think of anything else?

ALEX: Do you?

MAGDA: Yes, but ... in a different way. I keep thinking about our fear.

ALEX: What do you mean?

MAGDA: The woman said to me, while we were sitting there, 'I feel I've lost my body'. Do you know what I thought?

ALEX: You could help her find it again.

MAGDA: What rubbish! It made me think of the woman in my novel. Do you remember I told you, when she meets the unknown man she's petrified?

ALEX: People can be very kinky!

MAGDA: Why is she petrified? Wouldn't the normal thing be to run away?

She's meeting her rapist, not Romeo! But she stays there. Why does she stay?

ALEX: I wonder why!

MAGDA: What keeps her there is fear. She stays put, even though she is trembling, because she must face her fear. She is afraid, therefore she exists.

You would never understand! Give me a sip.

ALEX: (*gives her his glass*) Is that so? You've heard of course, about men's vaginal fear! Do you know about that fear? The womb's black darkness enveloping you? Then you talk about fear! You open your legs, and at the same time you're thinking about a dress you saw in a shop! We're born and die with that fear!

MAGDA: Sshhh, don't shout!

(*They remain silent ... * ALEX *goes to pour another drink ...* MAGDA *sits on the couch, stroking her body absent-mindedly.*)

MAGDA: One day I'll offer it to you.

ALEX: What? Which one?

MAGDA: My body. When I feel it inside my skin again, I'll make a gift of it to you. Then I'll spring up like a wild animal, in the throes of the big orgasm.

ALEX: Magda...

MAGDA: Oh, say it again, say it again!

ALEX: Magda, maybe we should go to a doctor?

MAGDA: My novel will cure me. Sometimes I feel a pulsation inside me, like the oriental sages, who called it a sign of intuitive wisdom ... or delusion, as you prefer. (*Jumps up suddenly, as if she's just remembered something.*) Is that why we kept changing bars? So we would meet your friend the shrink!

ALEX: That's really crazy!

MAGDA: I may be crazy too of course, you mean? You did everything you could, we went to five shitty bars, not for my sake, so that I would enjoy myself, but so that you could be with your buddy!

ALEX: We met him purely by chance.

MAGDA: You made it seem chance! The two of you kept on whispering, as if you were conspiring! Tell me what were you talking about?

Were you talking about crazy Magda?

ALEX: He was telling me about the woman in the bar!

MAGDA: I see, you were talking about whores then! About how you would screw all those whores you can't get!

ALEX: Now I see why you were pissed all the time we were together.

You don't dig him, do you? Why don't you say so then?

MAGDA: It's just that I don't like him. I don't like the way he stares at women!

ALEX: You know, you're really a laugh. You'd easily condemn him, just because he looks, you would even sue him for rape, just like that little bitch did to my client!

(*He sips his drink, goes to pour another, while* MAGDA *listens, and is extremely angry about what he is saying.*)

ALEX: She was in the club until four in the morning, had her fill of cocktails, wearing a cock-teaser mini-skirt, danced like a fury on the tables, and in the end, got into my client's car by her own choice, to go for a drive.
Then she pretends he raped her! You can bet I'll teach her a lesson!
'Tell us young lady, at which point exactly did the accused tear off your knickers? Or maybe you took them off yourself? Why don't you show the court what exactly happened? In what way did you put the condom on him, so that your rapist would not give you AIDS?'

MAGDA: (*in a fury*) Objection! Objection!

ALEX: You can make objections until kingdom come! I'll make her wish she never existed!

MAGDA: You're awful! You're dreadful!

ALEX: She lost her virginity at fourteen, with a friend of my client, who will testify.

MAGDA: Is it a crime for a girl to make love?

ALEX: The witness will testify, that it was the girl who persuaded him into doing it; actually she almost raped him!

MAGDA: The girl!

ALEX: Certainly! He will swear that she said 'If you don't screw me, I'll tell all the kids you can't get it up!'
You see? Psychological rape!

MAGDA: (*it's her turn to attack him now*) Is that so? Answer me Mr Defender: if your client was a good friend of your daughter, and your daughter went out with her friend, and the friend said he would take her home in his car, and on the way fucked the living daylights out of her, what would you do to him? Tell me what you would do!

ALEX: I would cut them off, and make him swallow them whole!

MAGDA: Do you want to know the rest?

ALEX: Stop it!

(MAGDA *happy as she goes on, but for* ALEX *each word is poison.*)

MAGDA: Today, on the excursion, Jenny made love for the first time with her boyfriend.

ALEX: Stop it!

MAGDA: My sweet child told me, and she was crying with joy. 'It was like flying, mummy,' she said, 'soaring high'.

ALEX: Stop it, stop it, stop it!

(ALEX *feels like doing something violent, breaking something, biting himself . . . in the end he goes to pour himself another drink. On his way back, he bumps into* MAGDA . . . *They remain looking at each other for a moment, then fall into each other's arms, crying . . . They kiss . . .* ALEX *becomes more and more passionate,* MAGDA *tries to escape . . . He throws her onto the couch, tears her clothes.*)

MAGDA: (*terrified*) No, darling, no! Please don't do it! I said no!
The child will hear you! . . . Stop! Don't! Stop! Don't . . . don't don't . . .

(ALEX *rapes her in a state of extreme anger, groaning. Slowly the lights go off in the sitting-room, and the scene is lit only by the dim light on the staircase . . .*
MAGDA *is sobbing, facing the public, as if asking for help . . .*
JENNY'S VOICE *is heard from upstairs.*)

JENNY'S VOICE: Mummy . . . Daddy, are you all right?

MAGDA: (*frantic and sobbing*) Yes, Jen! Yes, baby! Go to sleep!

JENNY'S VOICE: Goodnight.

MAGDA: Goodnight sweetheart! Sweet sea-dreams!

(*With a last groan,* ALEX *lets his weight fall on* MAGDA's *body, who is wracked by sobbing . . . But after that,* ALEX *sits up on the couch, and breaks into sobs too . . .*)

ALEX: Forgive me, Magda. Forgive me!

(*Darkness*)

SECOND PART

Sixth Scene

It's daytime. The phone rings. Once-twice-three times...
MAGDA comes home with the shopping, and runs to answer, but
hesitates, afraid ... the phone continues to ring, finally she picks
it up, anxiously.

MAGDA: Hello ... yes ... Who's speaking? Yes, speaking,
who are you?
Oh ... How can I help you? Well, I don't know much,
my husband ... Please calm down ... I understand
perfectly ... believe me, of course it's an extremely serious
matter ... What can I do? What can I possibly do? How
did things reach this stage? Tut, tut! Oh, my God! That's
incredible! I see, I see. I would like us to meet too, but not
just now please! What can I do, what can I say?
I believe you ... When? Now? Oh yes, then I must say
goodbye, so I won't miss it ... Thank you ... Keep your
courage up... (*She hangs up and hurries to turn on the*
television ... There is a live report outside the court. She is
facing the audience.)

REPORTER: Let's hear what the defence has to say. Is your
client innocent or guilty?

ALEX: The court will judge that. As always, we have
absolute trust in the unbiased judgement of our honest
and expert legal officers.

MAGDA: All this legal jargon!

REPORTER: There is a rumour that your client is rolling in
money. Is that true?

ALEX: I refuse to answer such low insinuations. My client is
a promising young man, you've seen him yourself,
descendant of a respectable family, a sustainer of the
human rights cause of...

MAGDA: They're all sustainers of some cause...

ALEX: and furthermore his father a candidate in this district in the forthcoming elections.

REPORTER: Do you believe every man is a potential rapist?

MAGDA: They only think of their cocks!

ALEX: Listen. All we civilians are victims, raped by the establishment, but if your assertion is valid, then the assertion that every woman is potentially a whore would also be valid, and that is something I abhor.

REPORTER: Some of the local people say that it's all a game of politics, and actually the girl is a victim of political competition.

ALEX: Sorry, but I don't pass judgement on television, only in court...

(*The report ends ...* MAGDA *turns off the television, and remains thoughtful ... From where she is sitting, her back is turned towards the door, so she doesn't see* ALEX *coming in ... She feels his presence though, and turns around in alarm.*)

MAGDA: Oh, I didn't hear you!

ALEX: Relax baby, relax! If I was the guy your heroine dreams of, you wouldn't be so frightened!

MAGDA: Sorry, I was lost in thought ... Tell me what happened, how did it go?

(*They kiss.*)

(MAGDA *helps him take off his coat, and puts down his briefcase and files.*)

ALEX: What do you think, shit. The trial hasn't started yet, and the vultures are already attacking with their cameras.

MAGDA: I just saw it.

ALEX: Oh, you saw it? How did you know? You never watch television.

MAGDA: (*lying of course*) I turned it on by chance.

(ALEX *makes questioning gestures in the direction of the upper-floor,* 'What's going on? How is Jenny?')

MAGDA: (*in a low voice*) She's upstairs. Studying, with her walkman on.

ALEX: (*the same*) Has she eaten?

MAGDA: Just a salad. (*In an apologetic tone*) I didn't cook today!

ALEX: That's a good start to stop eating.

(*Takes a bunch of banknotes out of his briefcase, and throws them onto the couch, on the table, anywhere . . .*)

MAGDA: So you got the money!

ALEX: I got the money, did the architect call? Why not build a swimming-pool as well? (*Lifts her up in his arms*) You can swim on a lilo, and write your thriller!

MAGDA: (*in a complaining tone*) I bet you don't want me even to write it!

ALEX: Why shouldn't I? It could become a serial too, and you'll be a literary lady, a bestselling writer!

MAGDA: (*showing she hurts somewhere*) Oh . . . Ouch!

ALEX: What's wrong with my baby? Is your head hurting? The mice again?

MAGDA: There's some demonic force in me. I can feel it in my whole body.
My body is telling me something, it's crying out, but I can't hear it yet. Have you had anything to eat?

ALEX: We had a snack at the bar.

MAGDA: At the bar for lunch?

ALEX: We went there with my client, to chat. Do you know what I discovered?
I'll have a drink. (*Goes to pour his drink*)

MAGDA: What? Good, bad?

ALEX: The son raped the girl, encouraged by his father.

MAGDA: I don't follow you.

ALEX: The youngster is a country bumpkin. The father instigated the rape.
From what the boy told me, and the little rascal is really a nice guy, he confessed that his father kept telling him 'go on, screw her, you jerk, can't you see she's asking for it'.

MAGDA: The bastard!

ALEX: So after the club, where they'd had their drinks of course, the fatal events took place. I need another sip myself. You know, we lawyers should be paid a special allowance for cleansing our salivary glands. Have you ever heard that before?

MAGDA: You are, aren't you? You get all that money.

ALEX: We get it, but we spend it too, baby. Here and there.

MAGDA: Like where?

ALEX: Darling, at trials by jury, most times the jury is on our side. How does that happen? Through the television channels. If you have even one judge on your side, and the jury as well, you've won the trial.

(*The phone rings.*)

MAGDA: Don't answer! (*Stands in his way*)

ALEX: Why, are we hiding?

MAGDA: Somebody keeps calling ... threatening you and swearing ... I can't bear hearing them! Don't answer, I'll disconnect it completely, you can use your mobile. Just now, the girl's mother called and begged me to tell you ...

ALEX: Tell me what, for chrissake, tell me what? Do you know why they reached court? The girl's father insisted, thinking that his political rival's son would be found guilty of rape, so he would win the elections.

MAGDA: Oh, my God! All these Iphigenias! So many! He raped her didn't he?

ALEX: Even if he's guilty, I must defend him, and if possible prove his innocence. Without humiliating the girl, don't worry. If her mother calls again tell her so.

MAGDA: That's right darling! Will you make it?

ALEX: Everything is possible. It will be a difficult game, but I think I'll win. I must.

MAGDA: By paying the TV channels?

ALEX: TV channels, bigwigs, they all have their own way of getting dirty money. But I refuse to do that. I will fight. Unfortunately darling, in this consumer society, the sole blind justice is money and power. They shove it with closed eyes, and threaten with masked faces.

MAGDA: Why don't you tell Jenny this too?

ALEX: I would dearly like to, but I can't. If I did, I would feel totally desparate. Right now, I still hope that we won't keep going from bad to worse.

I hope, therefore I exist, I exist, therefore I hope.

MAGDA: Aren't you telling her about the case?

ALEX: Of course I am!

MAGDA: Before she sees it on television, isn't it better?

ALEX: What do you think? That I should go upstairs and tell her joyfully 'I have a rape case, and I'm defending the rapist, so we can build a swimming pool?' Anyway, she didn't tell me either.

MAGDA: She will, when she feels like it.

ALEX: After how many condoms?

MAGDA: Aren't you ashamed of yourself?

ALEX: I am. I am even more ashamed, because I searched her handbag.

MAGDA: Really! That's the limit! What did you find? What great discovery did you make?

ALEX: Nothing ... Only a tiny little diary.

MAGDA: You read it!

ALEX: (*lying?*) No. I closed the handbag at once, I was so ashamed.

MAGDA: So you still have some feelings!

ALEX: Maybe you should.

MAGDA: No, I shouldn't!

ALEX: I say maybe you should read it some day.

MAGDA: I'll never read it. Is that clear?

ALEX: All right ... (*Some moments pass.*) Where are you?

MAGDA: Where would I be? I'm searching too, in my mind's handbag. I'm trying to see why this woman I'm writing about has this dream, and what stops her from remembering who the man is. Maybe she refuses to?

ALEX: What?

MAGDA: That's good. She refuses to remember the whole dream!

ALEX: Why?

MAGDA: Just like that ... because of fear. Fear of some revelation. I thought of making her fall in love with him ...

ALEX: Is that new?

MAGDA: Yes, I thought of it today. At the same time she

feels terror, she also feels in love with him. Isn't it nice?

ALEX: Like darkness in a tunnel. I have to rush to the toilet. I'll be back right away.

(*He goes inside ...* MAGDA *continues searching her mind, throws a glance in her notebook ... Suddenly she discovers something in her mind, and is alarmed.*)

MAGDA: Darling, come quickly! Run!

(*She lights a cigarette, has a sip ...* ALEX *arrives.*)

ALEX: What's wrong?

MAGDA: I had an image from the dream!

ALEX: Don't think any more, Magda! Relax!

MAGDA: It's a black form...

ALEX: You can't have an image from the dream, it's not you dreaming, it's a woman in your imagination! Come on!

MAGDA: (*pushes him away gently*) Don't touch me! Yes, it's crazy! I can't believe it!

ALEX: (*touches her again*) Magda...

MAGDA: (*almost angrily*) Don't touch me! Let me see clearly. (*closes her eyes*) Yes, yes, now I see clearly.

ALEX: Open your eyes and wake up! Wake up before we go crazy!

MAGDA: (*finally sees clearly*) Darling ... baby ... Alex ... I didn't imagine the novel! I dreamt it!

(ALEX *moves about nervously, tries not to show his desperation.*)

MAGDA: Do you remember I told you, I have dreams I can't remember? That's why I always wake up frantic ... That's why I feel my head's breaking!
That's why I lose myself! I'm scared! I'm terrified! Hold me!

(ALEX *embraces her gently from behind.*)

MAGDA: Just like that, I glimpse it for a second, and then it's gone. I try to grasp it in my sleep, and it slips further and further away ... Oh, my head feels relaxed. I'm numb all over! Give me a sip...

(ALEX *takes the glass, gives her a sip, lights a cigarette.*)

MAGDA: Thank you baby ... Another time, in another dream, he was behind me, pursuing me, and instead of running, I was petrified ... I was running in slow motion, and this stranger caught me, touched me, and his touch turned me on, excited me! I felt terror, and at the same time deep sexual desire! (*She almost laughs.*)

I thought I had a subject for a novel, and all the time the novel was myself. The dream became reality. But why? Why?

ALEX: Come on now, that's enough, stop.

MAGDA: In the long run, it's better like this, isn't it? Why should I keep trying to find what and why, an unknown woman dreams about. It's my own dream, and I use it as I like.

ALEX: Or it uses you. Shall we go inside?

MAGDA: What do you mean?

ALEX: What now?

MAGDA: What did you say the dream does to me?

ALEX: I didn't say anything.

MAGDA: No, it does, it does. It plays with me like cat and mouse. Like an elephant with an ant. There's an elephant hiding behind the ant! I'm scared!

ALEX: Don't be scared before fear-time arrives.

MAGDA: If it's here already?

ALEX: If it is ... it will show.

MAGDA: Touch me! I've never allowed any other man to touch me. I was afraid he would be electrocuted! But you touch me, if you want. If you're to be electrocuted, I have time to cut the wire, or pull out the plug, so you'll be saved.

ALEX: Shall we go inside?

MAGDA: Why inside?

(*The phone rings,* MAGDA *is alarmed, hugs him. At the third ring ... Darkness*)

Seventh Scene

*It's night-time ... The scene is lit by the table-lamp and the
light on the stairs ...* ALEX *enters on tiptoe ... Looks around,
then upstairs ... He goes abruptly inside, as if trying to hide
from somebody.* MAGDA *comes in too...
Puts another light on, takes off her coat, throws a glance upstairs
and towards the other rooms ... Has a glass of water and a
pill, turns the light off, and goes up the stairs ... disappearing
from view.*
ALEX *comes out again ... Takes off his coat and shoes, pours a
drink, lights a cigarette, turns off the table-lamp, lies down on
the couch, drinking and smoking...
The mobile, which he has put down on the table, rings ... He
answers, speaking in a whisper...*

ALEX: Yes ... yes ... what's up? Don't tell him anything
yourself. Let me talk to him ... He isn't ruining anything.
No, no ... A lawyer is a confessor, a father is padre-
padrone ... Where are you? Yes, all right, I'm coming...

(*He hangs up, gets up, turns on the lamp, looks at his watch,
puts on his shoes, takes* MAGDA's *notebook and writes
something, puts on his coat, takes the mobile, leaves the
notebook at the foot of the stairs, and goes out...
MAGDA comes down ... Sees the notebook, picks it up and
reads ... Leans on the wall...*)

(*Darkness*)

Eighth Scene

MAGDA *is sitting at her desk, typing ... She takes the page out,
glances at it and places it on top of the others ... Stretches her
muscles, which are cramped ... Then she gets up, takes her
mug, and goes to get some coffee...
Passing in front of the mirror, she looks at her body ... For the*

first time she touches it, with an expression close to pleasure . . .
Leaves the coffee mug on the desk, stretches again, and sits
down. Puts a page in the typewriter, and starts typing.
ALEX *comes home. Remains standing for a moment.*

ALEX: Don't be alarmed.

MAGDA: (*isn't alarmed*) Welcome home! (*Gets up for a kiss*)
Why should I be alarmed? Are you a bogey-man?

ALEX: How do I know what goes on in your mind? I see
you've started typing.

MAGDA: Nothing can stop me! There's a thriller in my
typewriter! Are you dead tired?

ALEX: You can say that again. I just want a coffee, please.

MAGDA: Why don't you have a shower? (*Turns off the music.*)

ALEX: Better not, my legs are shaking, I'll fall down in the
bath. In any case, I already got a cold shower from the
security systems engineer. We don't build houses nowa-
days, we build forts!

MAGDA: (*prepares his coffee*) In any case, I will fill the
balcony with every variety of flower!

ALEX: Beans and marrows?

MAGDA: Why are you sarcastic? They grow quickly, and
make a nice creeper. All right, I'll put jasmine and
honeysuckle for you. I got all the information from the
flower-arrangers. Look, I'm making a little posy, do you like
it? (*Shows him a big bouquet of artificial flowers, half-finished*)

ALEX: It looks pretty. You're really good with your hands!
(*Lights a cigarette*)

MAGDA: (*continues arranging the bouquet*) Did you sleep at
the office? I was worried when I read your note. What
happened?

ALEX: (*in a tired voice*) Something happened. I'll tell you
tomorrow, when there are further developments. Something happened with the youngster.

(MAGDA *talks non-stop,* ALEX *watches her, surprised and
irritated*)

MAGDA: You call the rapist a youngster? What did he do,

rape another girl? That's what they're like, once they start you can't stop them. They get even worse in prison. When they get out, they start all over again. We read about all that, don't we? Castration is the only answer. In war, you win if you disarm the enemy, it's the same with them. It's a weapon too, and extremely dangerous, as you very well know. That's why they rape women in wars; to kill them in a worse way, they humiliate a whole nation. Raped women mean a raped nation.

ALEX: What's wrong now? What's the matter? What are you raving about?

MAGDA: Raving? Was I raving? I was talking to you!

ALEX: Talking about what! Write all this in your thriller.

MAGDA: Well, you never tell me what happens in the big world outside.

ALEX: Did you see the news?

MAGDA: God forbid, what should I see? Rubbish?

ALEX: There was a demonstration today, outside the court. A women's organization.

MAGDA: Really? Good for them! If I weren't your wife, I would have gone myself.

ALEX: Why, don't lawyers' wives have a mind of their own?

MAGDA: They do, but can you imagine me demonstrating? What would happen, if somebody recognized me, and said 'What are you doing here Mrs Defender? Tell your husband first, start the revolution in your own home, and then in the streets'. Would they be wrong?

(ALEX *can't bear to listen, goes inside with his files,* MAGDA *continues . . .*)

MAGDA: They would be right. That's where every revolution should start. What use are people who go about shouting freedom and democracy, when in their homes they are the worst of fascists! (*Realizes she is alone . . . Wonders*) Am I raving? Shall I ring up for something to eat? Are you having a shower?

Oh, your psychiatrist friend called . . . Did he say anyhting about me? Am I well, or shall I start screaming?

(*Continues arranging the bouquet*)

We go out for the evening, and bang! there's the shrink, observing us, making a diagnosis! When they are the maddest of all!

ALEX: (*comes out again*) The shrink comes for me, Magda.

MAGDA: (*remains speechless, staring at him*) For you!

ALEX: For me. We meet every now and then, and chat. I disclose the dark corners of my soul to him.

MAGDA: (*approaches him tenderly*) What am I here for then? What am I for?

ALEX: It isn't easy, Magda. You know it yourself. You don't talk either.

MAGDA: Don't I talk?

ALEX: You rave, asleep and awake! That's what shrinks are for, so we can let off steam, because if we all talked openly to each other, there would be a massacre.

MAGDA: What's wrong, darling? What's the matter?

ALEX: Nothing ... You're looking for your thriller, and I'm looking for mine.

MAGDA: (*changes the subject casually*) Shall I tell you what I thought of today?

ALEX: Tell me.

MAGDA: So, I have the dream, but why did my 'inner voice' make it appear as a brainwave for a novel? Mm? Why couldn't I just wake up like every day, and remember my dream? No headaches or anything else. How do I know this is the first time I dreamt it, and I haven't been dreaming it for years, and forgetting? Mm? ... I did something bad today.

ALEX: What?

MAGDA: I searched Jenny's handbag. I'm sorry, but it's your fault ... You tempted me, I wanted to see what was written in her diary.

ALEX: You didn't find it, I bet.

MAGDA: How do you know?

ALEX: Well, if you had, you would have read it, you would tell me.

MAGDA: What would I tell you?

ALEX: Nothing. I told you, I only read a bit, from a page where she had written something about her dreams.

MAGDA: The seas, eh? What a good child we have! Sometimes I think how happy we must have felt that time we made love and little Jen was conceived! I wonder, do you remember exactly how it happened? I can't.

I keep wracking my brains to remember, no way! How could one remember after sixteen years! It was in my parents' house, right in the beginning, when my body still functioned. Do you still like my body?

ALEX: (*to close the discussion*) I like it Magda, I like it! What's got into you today, can you tell me?

MAGDA: Today I understood something our Jen often tells me. 'Mummy, you're a very elusive person'. I feel as if I've been absent for a long time. I travelled and travelled, and now I'm near the end ... 'Hope the voyage is a long one'. Well, it's certainly long, I must say!

(ALEX *stands over the typewriter, looking.*)

MAGDA: Don't, don't look! (*With an expression of self-importance*) A writer may talk with everybody, but when he writes, he's alone!

ALEX: Did I interrupt you at a crucial point?

MAGDA: No problem, there's not much to interrupt. (*Indicates her head*) Everything is inside here all the time! Every single moment! Last night after you left I was scared.

ALEX: What were you scared of? I left you a note, saying DON'T WORRY, I'M MEETING MY CLIENT ABOUT SOMETHING URGENT.

MAGDA: Yes, all right darling, but ... I thought maybe – forgive me, I'm not accusing you – I just wondered, maybe he's seeing another woman?

ALEX: (*calmly and convincingly*) There's no other woman, Magda.

MAGDA: After all these years?

ALEX: All these years. Just some silly, fleeting flirtations, already forgotten.

MAGDA: What was it like?

ALEX: (*nervously*) Like nothing! Lets drop the subject, it's not so easy for something to happen, love starts in the mind, and when the mind is confused, it confuses everything else too. You know all that.

MAGDA: Your mind in confusion? You, the holy terror of reason?

ALEX: Those are the ones you should fear most.

MAGDA: I'm not afraid of you, why should I be? Are you glad about Jen?

ALEX: You wouldn't believe it. I told the doctor too. I feel a weight off my mind, a worry, a burden. I feel I love her more deeply, better! I feel her inside me, I don't know what to say.

MAGDA: Before? How did you feel about her before?

ALEX: Distant, outside myself. Since the other day when ... I put her inside my heart, and I'm not losing her again.

MAGDA: Where am I, in your heart or faraway?

ALEX: In the depths in my heart!

MAGDA: Good?

ALEX: Good.

MAGDA: That's nice ... What happened with the youngster? You see, I called the little monster a youngster too.

ALEX: He keeps crying. I talked to him, calmed him down. But his father is furious. He's afraid he'll lose the game. He insisted I humiliate the girl tomorrow in court. He's even paid people to shout outside his political rival's house and office. You see, it's a small provincial society.

MAGDA: What will they be shouting?

ALEX: Can't you guess? Whore and that kind of thing.

MAGDA: What monsters! What are you going to do?

ALEX: I was thinking of asking Jenny to come to court tomorrow.

MAGDA: Never! I'm surprised you even thought of that. That Jen should come and hear you humiliating the girl!

ALEX: She'll hear something else ... I told the architect no swimming-pool, no alarm-system, no fence, no dogs, no ...

MAGDA: I don't want that either. I've got you, Jen, I've got everything.

ALEX: You've got your thriller too, silly girl.

MAGDA: Yes, I'll finish it, you'll see. Only I must find out who this man is, and what he wants.

ALEX: You'll find out, I'm sure.

MAGDA: Then it's finished!

ALEX: Yes, it's finished.

(*They embrace tenderly . . .*)

(*Darkness*)

Ninth Scene

In the dark, the aria 'E lucevan le stelle', from 'Tosca' is heard . . .
Dim evening lighting is turned on, and we see ALEX *sitting in*
an armchair, holding his head . . . In two minutes he gets up,
takes his glass and goes to pour himself a fresh drink . . . He
hesitates for a second, listens to the aria, picks up the remote
control, turns up the sound, listens carefully, turns it down,
pours a drink and comes back to the couch . . . Lights a
cigarette, and sits drinking, thinking and listening.
MAGDA *appears, in her dressing-gown.*

MAGDA: Are you sleeping here?

ALEX: Did I wake you?

MAGDA: No, no, I couldn't hear anything. Did you just come in?

ALEX: More or less. I was late in the office, and went for a drink afterwards.

Did you go out? Did you go to the movies as you had planned?

MAGDA: (*drinking water*) Yes, but I left as soon as the lights went off.

ALEX: Were you scared?

MAGDA: No, but I didn't want to fill my mind with other people's dreams.

My own are enough. You poor darling, what were you

thinking of, all alone here?

ALEX: To be or not to be.

MAGDA: Listening to 'Tosca', especially 'I never loved my life'?

ALEX: I like that part. I feel it digging up my whole being.

MAGDA: You'll find something, if you keep digging. So do I, but...

ALEX: I'm not digging, I'm discovering, Picasso would say. Did you have your pill?

MAGDA: I did, but I'm so tense, that instead of sleeping, I wake up even more tense. Would you like one?

ALEX: No ... I must wake up with a clear head tomorrow.

MAGDA: Depending on your dreams. Did you know that if somebody didn't dream for a week, they might die?

ALEX: Really?

MAGDA: Something happens to the brain, it explodes. Just think, all those wonderful or terrifying scenes we see every night, in our dreams, and then next morning there's nothing. Even though we don't remember a thing, if we didn't have those dreams, bang!

ALEX: Therefore dreams are a source of life.

MAGDA: Something like that. That's how I think of mine. It's happening, I say, to remind me of my body.

ALEX: (*goes to get a drink*) In what way?

MAGDA: The fear I feel in the dream, keeps my body alive. (*Referring to 'Tosca'*) This, this part I really adore! (*Picks up the remote-control and turns the sound up*) Listen! Don't worry, Jen is fast asleep. (*Repeats the line*) La vita ... Non ho amato mai la vita!

(*Turns it off abruptly, as soon as the applause begins*) It's really strange. An elephant hiding behind an ant, and yet we can't see it.

Don't stand behind me please.

ALEX: (*moves calmly*) Maybe you don't have to find it. Maybe you shouldn't...

MAGDA: (*preparing it*) Would you like a cup of relaxing cinnamon tea?

ALEX: No, I have a drink.

MAGDA: We didn't drink before, do you remember?

ALEX: Of course we did. We used to get drunk...

MAGDA: I never get drunk.

ALEX: You do. Anybody who drinks a lot, gets drunk.

MAGDA: Me too?

ALEX: You too. But next day you forget.

MAGDA: I get drunk?

ALEX: I meant in the past ... once or twice...

MAGDA: I don't remember.

ALEX: I know.

MAGDA: Do you remember everything perfectly?

ALEX: Oh no, I forget too. Then I remember, after some time, then I forget again ... The question is – to remember or not to remember?

Do you remember the other evening?

MAGDA: What?

ALEX: Here, on the couch ... at night.

MAGDA: I think I remember something.

ALEX: Forgive me...

MAGDA: Were you thinking about that, all alone here?

ALEX: That too.

MAGDA: I forgive, therefore I exist. On the other hand, maybe I was to blame too, I'm not sure ... (*Sips her tea*)

ALEX: Why should you be to blame, not at all!

MAGDA: You'd never done that before. I don't remember you doing it before.

ALEX: (*awkwardly*) Go and get some sleep, please. I want to sit here for a while, to think about tomorrow. I win or lose tomorrow.

MAGDA: Don't tell me. You can tell me when it's over. Jen found out.

Completely by chance. The girl, the victim, is a cousin of one of her classmates. Well, she told her.

ALEX: What did she say?

MAGDA: The cousin?

ALEX: Jenny.

MAGDA: The dear child was glad. Really proud!

ALEX: How come?

MAGDA: Her classmate said 'Your father is an excellent person. He didn't say one word against my cousin' I knew it. Do you think I believed what you were shouting the other night? A lot of things are said and done, when we're angry or drunk. I know you, don't I?

ALEX: Do you know me?

MAGDA: (*looks at him wondering*) Of course I know you. Are we playing a thriller-game?

ALEX: Life is a game, and if you don't play you lose.

MAGDA: Am I playing?

ALEX: It's your thriller.

MAGDA: Then I'll win. Haven't I been telling you all this time?

ALEX: Go to bed.

MAGDA: I'm going, now. (*Drinks the last sips of her tea*) I thought of something else this afternoon.

ALEX: What?

MAGDA: About the man in my nightmares.

ALEX: What?

MAGDA: I can't grasp it, I can't understand, I can't ... don't stand behind me, darling!

ALEX: You keep moving in front of me, I haven't moved all this time.

MAGDA: Sorry, I'm going. Will you be late?

ALEX: No. You go to sleep.

MAGDA: A kiss?

(*They kiss gently.*)

MAGDA: Sweet dreams

ALEX: Sweet dreams

MAGDA: (*leaves happily*) Seas, seas ... (*Before leaving the room, she hesitates, looks back.*) I'll tell you. Did you ever think it might be you?

ALEX: Me? Who?

MAGDA: Him ... On the other hand, I tell myself, if it's you, why can't I see you clearly, why do you always hide, why always in the dark? It's all confused, dreamlike ... nightmarish. Tomorrow you win or lose? Eh?

ALEX: Yes.
MAGDA: Good luck, darling. Goodnight.
ALEX: Goodnight.
MAGDA: Don't drink any more.

(*She leaves the room* ... ALEX *finishes the rest of his drink in one gulp* ... *Stands still, thoughtful*...)

(*Darkness*)

Tenth Scene

Evening ... MAGDA *comes home* ... *Calls, while putting on the lights.*

MAGDA: Alex! Jenny! Jenny darling! (*Takes her coat off etc. Looks at her watch* ... *Dials a number on the phone*)
Yes ... Hello dear, it's Magda, everything all right? ... Mr Alex? Oh ... oh ... Oh ... How come you're still there at this time? I haven't heard anything, no calls either, I wanted everything to be over first. Really? Oh, that's good news! Yes, yes, I'll turn it on now. Thank you dear, have a nice evening.

(*Hangs up, goes quickly to the television and turns it on, lights a cigarette*...
Sits down, impatient to watch ... *A well-known anchor-man on the 8.15 evening news*...
During the opening scenes, a 'split screen' may be shown, with data-bank images from the courts, featuring unidentifiable faces and events...)

ANCHOR-MAN: Now, ladies and gentlemen, let's see today's events. There have been unexpected developments in the rape case trial in the criminal court. Suddenly and unexpectedly, the accused young man confessed his action, asked forgiveness from the victim, whom he referred to as 'my childhood sweetheart' and then pro-ceeded to propose marriage to her, which was accepted by the plaintiff with joy, and was applauded by the court.

MAGDA: Bravo, bravo, bravo.

ANCHOR-MAN: Following this dramatic conclusion, we go live to the defence lawyer, who agreed to have a few words exclusively with us.

(ALEX *appears in the 'split-screen'*.)

ANCHOR-MAN: Good evening. Can you hear me?

ALEX: Good evening. Of course I can hear you.

MAGDA: So can I, so can I!

ANCHOR-MAN: What is your opinion about your client's extraordinary and unexpected behaviour?

ALEX: Well ... I think my client proved himself a paragon of maturity. Not only his public plea for forgiveness to the young lady in question, but also his honest and extremely sensitive proposal of a life-union between them, as two free and loving persons, demonstrates not only a *de profundis* repentance, but also a concsious choice towards more noble and humane ideals. We are living in hard times, and it is highly probable that someone may become the victim of false ideals and modes of behaviour, and I believe that justice, in cases like my client's, acts correctly in applying an open and attentive mind to the situation, so as to ...

ANCHOR-MAN: ... and justly adjourned the trial.

Another factor which impressed public opinion was the course of action adopted by the defence. We all know that in a rape-case, the defence unfortunately – I repeat – unfortunately – is mainly based on humiliating the victim's character. Not only did you avoid humiliating the girl, but on the contrary, you defended a rapist, while at the same time defending the female character in general, and the specific girl's in particular.

ALEX: I think that it is time for the rapist be considered like any other criminal, i.e. in a murder case we do not abuse the victim's body, saying that he asked for it, but we punish the murderer, the same way as in a bank robbery, we do not say that the bank is guilty of having money in the vaults, having thus provoked the robber.

ANCHOR-MAN: It has been said that your client's decision is due mainly to your advice...

ALEX: My client understood his mistake, and I believe that true repentance always deserves to be pardoned. I forgive, therefore I exist.

MAGDA: Yes darling, yes! I'm listening!

ANCHOR-MAN: All right then, we can conclude at this point. All's well that ends well. Oh, one last question: Will the two fathers still be rivals in the upcoming election?

ALEX: I don't know about that. In any case, in church they will be in-laws.

ANCHOR-MAN: Good. We will be there too, to taste the wedding-cake of peace. Thank you very much and goodnight.

ALEX: Thank you too, goodnight.

MAGDA: Come on, come on! (*Turns off the TV, goes to pour a drink...*)

(*The phone rings, she runs to answer.*)

MAGDA: Yes ... yes dear, I saw it! No, daddy isn't back yet ... Will you be late?
All right, we'll wait for you to celebrate afterwards ... yes, yes, I love you. (*Hangs up ... wishes* ALEX *was there*) Where are you? Where are you?

(*The door is heard closing loudly, she's glad.*)

MAGDA: You're here! Alex!

(*She runs happily to welcome him ... We hear voices, and in two minutes they enter,* MAGDA *almost dragging a drunken* ALEX.)

MAGDA: Come on darling ... just a little more ... hold on ... just one little step ... there's my baby ... here we are!
(*Lets him fall onto the couch*)

ALEX: (*with drunken arrogance*) Drrrink! Please!

MAGDA: I'll make you some camomile-tea.

ALEX: Drrink! Please ... little miss ant!

MAGDA: I beg your pardon! Take your coat off ... put those damned files down ... take off your shoes...

ALEX: Drrink! A drink for the elephant! Please!

MAGDA: Now you're talking Greek, all right . . . lie down, lie down.

Would you like some music?

ALEX: *Non ho amato mai la vita!*

MAGDA: Digging again? It's late now, you're tired.

ALEX: (*intensely*) I'm not tired, I'm drunk!

MAGDA: So what? You just had a bit too much.

ALEX: Much more! As much as an elephant!

MAGDA: (*threatens him jokingly*) Listen darling. I'll leave you to sleep here, and when Jen comes back, she'll find you in this awful state.

ALEX: Where is she?

MAGDA: With her friends. They saw you on television. They were really happy. So was I. I was almost in tears!

ALEX: You were almost in tears were you? Now you'll cry for sure! (*He takes her in his arms tightly, lovingly, almost crying.*)

MAGDA: What's wrong darling? Don't scare me! Calm down!

(ALEX *lets her go, gets up staggering, goes to get a drink.*)

MAGDA: Where are you going? Not another one! Don't drink any more!

ALEX: Too late now! Now the digger has discovered the corpse! It's time for the exhumation, to discover the real causes of death.

MAGDA: Stop it! I'm scared!

ALEX: The time of fear has arrived, darling! I told you so from the start, didn't I? I told you, write a different novel.

MAGDA: I won't write it, I've decided not to. I'm not interested in writing it any more.

ALEX: But you must find it. You can't turn back now. We've reached hell. (*Drinks*) Who is the man, Magda? Look at me! Dream of me! Do I remind you of anybody?

MAGDA: (*can't bear any more, is in hysterics*) Stop! (*Turns her back to him*)

ALEX: Your mind had almost revealed the truth, but you denied it. You thought I might be the dark man in your nightmares? Didn't you?

MAGDA: (*feels lost, searches inside her mind ... searches*) Yes, but it isn't you! Why should it be you? Don't stand behind me! Get away from behind me! (*Remembers, is frantic*) Don't! No! Yes! It's you!
(*Turns and looks at him*) Yes ... The darkness is gone ... It's you! YOU!

(*She beats his chest,* ALEX *remains still, crying...*)

ALEX: I love you, Magda.

MAGDA: Why why why! Why do you keep haunting me! How many years have you been haunting me? What do you want from me? What do you want?

ALEX: Hit me, darling, hit me!

MAGDA: (*leaves him, crying...*) Why why why?

ALEX: Forgive me darling! Forgive me...

MAGDA: Why why why ... why couldn't I find you, why?

ALEX: Because then you would find the rest, too.

MAGDA: The rest? What else?

ALEX: Your rape.

MAGDA: (*is dumbfounded*) Whaaat! What rape?

ALEX: We came home drunk, and you were in some kind of hysterical isolation, you didn't even want me to touch you, but I desired you so much, you kept on refusing, pushing me away, and then I hit you, we fought, I threw you on the floor, and raped you, while you were half-conscious.
Then I put you to bed, and the next day when you woke up, you couldn't remember anything.

MAGDA: (*can't believe all this*) Impossible! Impossible! That could never happen, no! I can't believe it! Must I believe it? If I believe it ... when did this happen? When?

ALEX: It's the time you're trying to remember, but can't, you don't want to ... When Jenny was conceived.

MAGDA: (*dumbfounded*) When Jenny was conceived? Jen? Do you mean little Jen...

ALEX: (*in anguish too*) Yes Magda. Jen is the child of your rape.

MAGDA: No! (*Hits him*) No no no! (*Heartbroken*) Why? Why are you telling me, why? Oh my God! It's as if my womb is being torn apart!

I feel as if I'm giving birth! As if Jen is coming out of me once more, the way she is now! My baby!

ALEX: I had to Magda. For you and for me. From the moment you started describing your thriller, my whole being was in torment. On the one hand I didn't want you to remember, I was afriad ... on the other I wanted it, this torment had to end after all these years!

MAGDA: All these years, you knew, you remembered? How could you bear it?

How could you bear it? All these years I was dead by your side, and you could work, have a career, sleep with me, hear me crying, touch me, talk to me, pet me and let me pet you and love you like I never loved myself!

How could you bear it?

ALEX: I buried everything deep inside myself too. Sometimes I remembered, others I pushed everything away. Your thriller made me anxious. I discussed it with the doctor. He helped me realize, that finally the moment had arrived for you to remember or lose yourself.

MAGDA: How could I forget everything! My cries, my sobbing, my pleas!

Absolute silence of the grave! I buried my soul and my body! Beast!

The other day you did it again, and I was begging you, so that Jen wouldn't hear. Beast beast beast!

ALEX: I wanted to get it over, Magda! I wanted to make you remember, even if that meant hurting you once more. I couldn't bear to see you tormenting yourself every day; it drove me mad! I love you, Magda.

MAGDA: I had even forgotten my name! Everything! Everything was a nightmare! Your black nightmarish shadow kept stalking me, day and night.

Until I lost my wits, and thought that unknown rapists and murderers were after me. It was you! The last time, I turned my head and saw you. But I kept telling myself, 'Why should it be him, it can't be him, I must be wrong!'. Suddenly I lost you. When I came home, I felt as if you had just come in, but I was afraid to look for you. Something made me stop.

ALEX: I was afraid for you, Magda. I didn't want anything else to hurt you. I didn't know where all that soul-searching would lead. I thought of really scaring you, to make you remember. That's why I told you to read Jenny's diary. She had written somewhere, 'Last night Daddy slept in the office, and I heard Mummy crying out in the night: Go away Alex, don't haunt me any more! I wonder what Mummy dreams about?'

MAGDA: My dear little girl! Flesh and blood of my flesh and blood! That's why you were afraid for Jen. You had your reasons to be afraid.

(*Both of them have relaxed ... MAGDA touches her body ... Moments pass...*)

MAGDA: Did we massacre each other?

ALEX: What?

MAGDA: You said that when people tell each other every-thing, it's a massacre.
Was it?

ALEX; No.

MAGDA: We lost time, though, didn't we?

ALEX: We found it.

(*They have approached each other ... JENNY'S VOICE is heard from outisde.*)

JENNY'S VOICE: Mummy, Daddy, we're here ... I'll just say goodnight to the kids.

(*A few moments of silence*)

MAGDA: Do you love me?

ALEX: I love you.

MAGDA: Sweetly?

ALEX: Sweetly.

MAGDA: Sweet seas!

ALEX: Sweet seas, darling.

(*Darkness*)

Eleventh Scene

It's daybreak ... MAGDA, *dressed to go out, is putting the last items in a suitcase ... places the cover on the typewriter, and puts it away in a cupboard, tears up two or three sheets of paper – the ones she had written – and throws them them in the waste-paper basket ...* ALEX *enters, half awake, in his dressing-gown ... Looks around...*

ALEX: What are you doing?

MAGDA: Packing a suitcase.

ALEX: You're packing at daybreak? Why may I ask?

MAGDA: I'm thinking of leaving.

ALEX: Leaving? Going where?

MAGDA: I had a dream...

ALEX: (*irritated*) Another dream!

MAGDA: I dreamt of my parents' house in ruins, and I thought I'd go and check.

ALEX: Check what, the ruins?

MAGDA: It's a good chance to get the mice out.

ALEX: (*nervously tries to stop her*) Hold on a minute, give me a chance.

What on earth are you talking about?

MAGDA: I just told you. I want to go away for a while.

ALEX: Suddenly like that?

MAGDA: Suddenly is never suddenly.

ALEX: What about Jenny?

MAGDA: What about Jenny? She's a grown woman now. She's got a home and a father, what's the problem? The fridge is stocked, the clothes are washed, the bills have been paid...

ALEX: So you had planned it?

MAGDA: (*softening a little*) Oh, leave me alone!

ALEX: I don't understand. What will you do all alone? Write your thriller?

MAGDA: That's over.

ALEX: So what will you do?

MAGDA: Nothing.

ALEX: Nothing?

MAGDA: Nothing. I don't want to do anything. Isn't that nice?

ALEX: (*sarcastically*) Wonderful! How long will you be away?

MAGDA: I don't know, I'll be away.

ALEX: (*asks her, but doubtfully*) Alone?

MAGDA: (*laughs sadly*) Do you suspect me, darling? Come on! I'm not going with somebody else. Now that I think of it, you never know what might happen. I may come back with somebody else.

ALEX: Magda...

MAGDA: What else can I say? Do you think I'm in the mood for love affairs? Now? That would really mean 'I'm bursting from health'!

ALEX: Or that we're mad.

MAGDA: (*meaning they're saved*) At the last minute!

ALEX: Do you think you'll find a ship at this hour?

MAGDA: 'There's no ship for you, there is no road'. I'll wait. It will be nice now, on the quay. I'll walk up and down, I'll watch the cargo-ships, the seagulls ... A sea-voyage at daybreak will be beautiful. The sea, the sea!

ALEX: I'll get dressed and drive you.

MAGDA: You don't want to drive me, you want to bring me back.

I've called a taxi. Go back to bed.

ALEX: (*tries to hold on to something*) Have you told Jenny?

MAGDA: You tell her.

ALEX: What am I supposed to tell her?

MAGDA: The truth.

ALEX: (*furious*) Fuck the bloody truth! What truth are you talking about?

Which truth?

(*A car is heard hooting.*)

MAGDA: Oh, that's the taxi. I must leave.

(*She shuts the suitcase ... goes to put on her coat ...* ALEX *watches her, almost exploding...*)

ALEX: (*finally stops her*) You're not going anywhere!

MAGDA: (*resists, calmly and decisively*) Alex ... please ... I must go.

ALEX: You're not going! (*Pulls her by the coat*)

MAGDA: (*intensely*) Let go!

ALEX: You're not going! (*Takes her coat off, by force*)

(*Two hoots*)

MAGDA: You'll wake the whole neighbourhood! You'll wake Jen!

ALEX: Let them wake up, just like we did!

MAGDA: Let them wake by themselves, not because of us. Let go!

ALEX: Put the suitcase down!

MAGDA: Alex, listen ... listen to me, it's important! Listen to me! You've never listened to me, I've got a voice too! I can't go on crying in silence, I can't go on crying forever in my dreams!

ALEX: Your dreams are driving us mad, can't you see?

MAGDA: They're mine and I love them! That's how they are, and I love them! I was born with them, and I love them! I grew up with them, and I love them! Let me go, please!

ALEX: Not one step!

MAGDA: (*furious*) Let me go, let me go, let me go!

(*She rushes at him and hits him ... ALEX hits back ... they struggle relentlessly ... He tears her clothes, she bleeds ... MAGDA grabs an object and hits him on the head ... ALEX falls on the floor ... Three hoots are heard ... MAGDA, breathing heavily, wipes the blood, arranges her torn dress as well as she can, puts her coat on, picks up the suitcase, goes to the door ... ALEX moves, showing that he isn't seriously injured ...*
Before going out, MAGDA turns and looks at him ...)

MAGDA: The thriller is over.

(*She goes out ... ALEX recovers, sits on the couch, lights a cigarette ...*

Suddenly JENNY'S VOICE *is heard, from upstairs, frightening*
ALEX ... *He smooths his hair and clothes.*)

JENNY'S VOICE: Daddy...

ALEX: You frightened me darling! Are you awake?

JENNY'S VOICE: Yes ... I had a nightmare. Is Mummy all right?

ALEX: Fine darling, fine. Go to sleep.

JENNY'S VOICE: I'm going. Tomorrow is another day.

ALEX: (*his voice is barely audible*) ... Yes, another day.

   (*Darkness*)

The End

With Power from Kifissia

by

Dimitris Kehaidis and Eleni Haviara

Translated by
Nelli Karra

The Characters

ALEKA.

ELECTRA.

FOTINI.

MARO.

ALEKA's *house in Kifissia. Combined sitting-room and kitchen. Stairs leading up to the bedrooms. A garden in front. Evening.* ALEKA *is working out on a cycling machine. She is wearing a gym suit.*

ALEKA: (*counting*) 106 ... 107 ... 108...

(*The sound of a motorcycle parking.* ELECTRA *enters.*)

ELECTRA: Well, well. What do we have here? (*She throws her bag and helmet on the couch. She takes off her jacket.*)

ALEKA: 112, 113, 114...

ELECTRA: Any calls for me?

ALEKA: 118 ... 119 ... 120...

ELECTRA: It has a counter. Don't wear yourself out.

ALEKA: 126 ... 127 ... 128...

ELECTRA: Is there anything to eat? (*She opens the refrigerator.*)

ALEKA: 132 ... 133 ... 134...

ELECTRA: What's going on here?

ALEKA: 136 ... 137 ... 138...

ELECTRA: No cheese ... no bread ... no ham ... no nothing. Where'd all that stuff go, Mom?

ALEKA: I threw it out. So I wouldn't be tempted ... 150 ... 151 ... 152...

ELECTRA: Oh, no, Mom ... you started that diet again ... You started that diet ... And now what am I supposed to eat?

ALEKA: There's boiled chicken.

ELECTRA: Boiled chicken? You know I don't eat boiled chicken.

ALEKA: Eat eggs.

ELECTRA: I'll eat eggs, eggs we have, eggs it is. What else can I do? I'll make some French fries...

ALEKA: Don't get your hopes up. There're no potatoes.

ELECTRA: There're no potatoes?

ALEKA: I got rid of the potatoes. I threw them out.

ELECTRA: Will someone please tell me what's to be done with you?

ALEKA: It's a crash diet. Because the doctor asked me, 'Do you want to diet, or do you want a crash diet?' I tell him. 'A crash diet because I'm in a hurry. I'm going on a trip soon.' Why are you looking at me like that, Electra? My mind's made up.

ELECTRA: I get the message (*She starts breaking the boiled eggs one by one.*)

(ALEKA *jumps up.*)

ALEKA: What are you doing? Why are you cracking those eggs?

ELECTRA: Didn't you say there're eggs?

ALEKA: What on earth are you doing?

ELECTRA: And that one's boiled ... And that one's boiled ... And that one's boiled...

ALEKA: Are you crazy?

ELECTRA: I'm looking for eggs to make an omelet.

ALEKA: What omelet? All those eggs are boiled.

ELECTRA: So what am I supposed to eat?

ALEKA: 'I want fried eggs ... I want French fried potatoes' ... To whom are you speaking of French fries? To a person who is dieting? And you know that French fries are my special weakness, I am crazy about French fries. And here you are talking to me about French fries. Go eat out.

ELECTRA: I don't want to eat out.

ALEKA: At other times you know how to eat out. Today you don't want to eat out. Because you're waiting for a call from that idiot ... (*Pause*) 'Jason's looking for a sponsor' ... 'To make a movie' ... That'll be a piece of crap too. Like his last one.

ELECTRA: What about his last one? His last one won an award.

ALEKA: Yeah, at that stupid festival.

ELECTRA: Where?

ALEKA: At Drama, wherever.

ELECTRA: No, no, it's not 'wherever'

ALEKA: And where are you shooting this film?

ELECTRA: I don't know, we'll see.

ALEKA: Because this house is, of course, out of the question.

ELECTRA: We'll see about that.

ALEKA: No, we won't see about that. No film crew is setting foot in here again. It cost me 1.5 million drachmas last time just to get this house back to normal. The workmen were stunned. They kept saying 'Jesus, Christ ... would you look at that?' Are you listening to me?

ELECTRA: OK, OK, stop shouting.

ALEKA: And don't think you'll get away with it at the last minute, That's not going to happen.

ELECTRA: Stop shouting, for chrissake.

ALEKA: Look who you fell in love with.

ELECTRA: It doesn't matter. At least you fell in love with a great artist.

ALEKA: I'm through with him.

ELECTRA: Yeah ... sure you're through.

ALEKA: I'm through. He didn't call me on my birthday – I'm through.

ELECTRA: That remains to be seen. (*She goes to the cassette player. She looks through the cassettes.*)

ALEKA: Oh my God! I'm starting to get hungry! The central nerve controlling my appetite has become stimulated now. Oh shit! I have to hold out though ... I have to hold out.

ELECTRA: Don't worry. You'll be forgetting your hunger any second now.

ALEKA: If I can hold out for just one minute it'll pass. (*Pacing up and down. Suddenly*) Lettuce! I'll eat lettuce.

ELECTRA: Any second now. Just you wait.

ALEKA: You little witch! (*She opens the refrigerator.*) Lettuce, where's the lettuce ...

(ELECTRA *puts a cassette into the recorder.*)

ELECTRA: Now just listen to him here ...

(*From the recorder comes Stefano's voice, singing an aria.* ALEKA *is eating lettuce.*)

ELECTRA: Do you hear that?

ALEKA: That's his worst tape...

ELECTRA: Did you catch the voice cracking there?

ALEKA: You know why. His voice here is tense because we had fought just that very evening and the man was distraught.

ELECTRA: Listen, just listen to that.

ALEKA: If it's Stefano's voice you want, play 'Forza dell Destino.' 'Forza dell Destino.'

ELECTRA: No. Whenever you get hysterical, this is what I'll play.

ALEKA: There! Now his voice is coming through. Listen ... just listen to that ... That crescendo ... Listen, it's rising now ... it's rising ... There, that's Stefano's voice! Is that a cracked voice? Is it? Listen ... It's going up again ... Rising...

(ELECTRA *laughs.*)

ALEKA: Watch now, just see how long he holds this high note!

ELECTRA: You are incredible!

ALEKA: That high note goes on forever!

(*The doorbell rings.*)

ALEKA: Oh! That's Maro and Fotini. Oh, dear and I'm not ready. What time is it?

ELECTRA: Eight thirty.

ALEKA: Turn it off. Turn it off. Quick.

(ELECTRA *turns off the cassette player.* ALEKA *opens the door.* FOTINI *enters in a rage.*)

ALEKA: Come on in. I need a minute to shower.

FOTINI: Forget the shower.

ALEKA: Just a quick shower.

FOTINI: More important things are happening.

ALEKA: Where's Maro?

FOTINI: Maro threw me out.

ALEKA: She threw you out?

FOTINI: She threw me out.

ALEKA: You mean Maro's not coming?

FOTINI: She says she's coming ... I'm not sure any more ... How should I know? She might not come. After what's happened...

ALEKA: Why wouldn't she come?

FOTINI: We're naïve, my dear. You and I are naïve.

ALEKA: Why, what happened?

FOTINI: She's lying to us that's what.

ALEKA: Be more specific, would you?

FOTINI: But I caught her, the cunt. I caught her in the act.

ALEKA: Tell me what's happened, dear. You're all over the place.

FOTINI: What can I tell you? Didn't we say we'd go to a movie?

ALEKA: That's what we said.

FOTINI: That we'd be here at 8.30.

ALEKA: Right. So, where's Maro?

FOTINI: Just listen. I pass by at 8.15 to pick her up to come here.

ALEKA: So...

FOTINI: I was even five minutes late, and I got there at twenty past. I ring the bell. She doesn't open the door. I say, what's going on? There's a light on inside ... I call 'Maro, Maro' ... And suddenly the door opens. And there she is! What can I tell you? In such a state. An indescribable state. She was dazed.

ALEKA: Dazed?

FOTINI: Totally. And red hot. Completely on fire! Steaming!

ALEKA: On fire? What do you mean on fire?

FOTINI: I went to touch her hand for a second and it was steaming hot. Her eyes were glazed ... so I say: Are you ready? And she says. 'Give me a couple of minutes.' I go to step inside – she pushes me back out.

ALEKA: What?

FOTINI: Exactly that, she pushes me back out and says 'Leave leave, and I'll be there...'

ALEKA: What do you mean 'leave, leave and I'll be there?'

FOTINI: I say 'What do you mean leave, leave, and I'll be there? Is there a reason?' She says 'I can't talk now – leave, leave and I'll be there.' I say 'Aren't we going to a movie?' 'We'll go, we'll go. Just leave and I'll be there.'

ALEKA: For goodness sake!

FOTINI: 'What's with you?' I say. 'Has something happened?' She says, 'I can't tell you now' and something I didn't catch . . . and 'I'll tell you later' . . . and she closes the door on me.

ALEKA: She closed the door on you?

FOTINI: She closed the door right in my face.

ALEKA: What's that all about?

FOTINI: I'll tell you what that's about . . . she's given in to Fatso.

ALEKA: To Fatso?

FOTINI: She's succumbed to Fatso. And most probably they were making love at that moment.

ALEKA: What?

FOTINI: I'm telling you she was steaming hot.

ALEKA: Don't say that. I don't want to believe it.

FOTINI: And her eyes were glazed.

ALEKA: I don't believe it.

FOTINI: Aside from the fact that I think I spotted his jacket . . .

ALEKA: Which one?

FOTINI: The plaid one. Doesn't Fatso have a plaid jacket?

ALEKA: Brown and beige.

FOTINI: That's what it looked like.

ALEKA: Oh my God! Are you sure?

FOTINI: Now that I think about it, I'm sure.

ALEKA: Oh, my God . . .

FOTINI: Because just as I turn to leave Fatso's jacket catches my eye . . . it was towards the back.

ALEKA: You saw Fatso's jacket?

FOTINI: Hanging on the coat rack. I saw it.

ALEKA: You mean Fatso was inside?

FOTINI: That's what I've been trying to tell you all this time. That Fatso was inside.

ALEKA: So what happens now?

FOTINI: You see?

ALEKA: Oh, my God...

FOTINI: She gave in to Fatso.

ALEKA: The stupid cunt.

FOTINI: Why wouldn't she let me in? Instead of 'Leave, leave and I'll be there?' Because she knew. If I were to catch her with Fatso – I'd be so furious – I'd belt her one.

(ALEKA *lights a cigarette.*)

ALEKA: She gave in to Fatso. The stupid cunt.

ELECTRA: What's it to the two of you, whatever she does?

FOTINI: What did you say, Electra?

ELECTRA: So what if she did sleep with Fatso? Why should she account to the two of you for it?

FOTINI: But you don't know what we've had to put up with because of him...

ELECTRA: What you've had to put up with?

ALEKA: Of course. It affects us as well.

ELECTRA: How?

FOTINI: And come to think of it, just three days ago she was screaming, 'It's over with Fatso. I'm through with him' ... And now this.

ELECTRA: Fine. So what?

ALEKA: Well, now she'll start all over again: 'What's going to happen with Fatso? What am I going to do with him?'

FOTINI: Exactly.

ALEKA: And then she'll start playing her tragedy of despair and longing.

FOTINI: And she'll harp on it for hours and days on end. She'll ask us, 'What do you think?' Over and over. 'Should I call? – shouldn't I call? ... should I call? – shouldn't I call? ... should I call? – shouldn't I call?' And then afterwards she'll say, 'I should cut off my arm for calling. If I so much as put a finger on that phone again I want you to cut it off' ... and that goes on forever!

ALEKA: Now do you understand, Electra?

ELECTRA: Well, so what? It's a special relationship.

FOTINI: Special relationship not withstanding, just wait until you see what's in store for her now.

ALEKA: The stupid cunt...

FOTINI: All hell's going to break loose.

ALEKA: She gave in, the idiot!

FOTINI: Because, my dear, you cannot cop out and upset the rest of us. We've made decisions here. To meet life head on, for chrissake. And here I am running from one travel agency to the next arranging our trip ... (*To* ALEKA) You said you'd end it with Stefano – you said it and you did it.

ALEKA: I did it.

FOTINI: Come to think of it, you were listening to him on the sly when I got here. That's suspect.

ALEKA: It's over I'm telling you...

FOTINI: But you said you destroyed the cassettes.

ALEKA: I did...

FOTINI: Yes, but he was singing away when I got here.

ALEKA: That's how Electra gets her kicks. She's sadistic.

FOTINI: Well, anyway. You said you'd end it – you ended it. Just wait and see what's in store for the other one who hasn't ended it. Because she'll show up any minute now saying, 'Jacket, what jacket? Fatso's jacket?' And then she'll blow off the trip.

ALEKA: No way.

FOTINI: And she'll want us to go see a vampire movie.

ALEKA: Which one?

FOTINI: *A Touch of Evil.* That one. I will not see movies like that.

ELECTRA: Why not?

FOTINI: They affect me ... Afterwards I have nightmares. Last night I had another nightmare. This chicken the size of a building. Don't laugh Electra ... It terrifies me...

ELECTRA: Anyway, it's not a vampire movie. It's an Orson Welles' film.

FOTINI: It's a thriller ... I will not go see thrillers any more. She's crazy about thrillers. She devotes herself to making that jewellery ... her nervous system is numb and she

needs thrillers to revive her. Well, I do not need reviving.
I'm already wired.

ELECTRA: (*hugs and kisses her*) That's my girl!

(*Doorbell*)

FOTINI: There she is, that's her! Or were you expecting
someone else?

ALEKA: No. No one.

FOTINI: That's her . . . (*She lights a cigarette.*)

(ALEKA *opens the door.* MARO *enters. She's holding a yellow
rose.*)

MARO: Hello, my darlings.

FOTINI: (*to* A) I, at any rate will discuss it no further. I will
make no agreements. I'll voice no objections. Nothing. I
will do as I please. And no one dare tell me what to do
with my life. (*She's shaking from head to foot.*)

ALEKA: Really now, there's no need for that.

MARO: What's with her?

ALEKA: (*to* F) Calm down.

FOTINI: I'm having a nervous breakdown.

ALEKA: Calm down.

FOTINI: I am having nervous breakdown at this very moment.

ALEKA: Shall I bring you a Valium?

FOTINI: I can't take any more of this. I'm under pressure.

ALEKA: Electra, where do we keep the Valium?

FOTINI: You're too late darling – I took one before I left the
house. Because we were going to a vampire movie. That's
one. And then when she threw me out I went into the
garden to that little faucet where she waters her flowers –
and I took another one.

ALEKA: Well then you'll soon be calmer.

MARO: Threw her out? Who threw her out?

ALEKA: The Valium will take effect and you'll feel calmer.

FOTINI: Yeah . . . Now she'll start telling things her way.
Don't forgive her . . . Don't forgive her . . .

MARO: I don't understand. What's going on?

FOTINI: 'Leave, leave and I'll be there. Leave, leave and I'll be there.' Who do you think you're talking to?

MARO: Who said 'Leave, leave and I'll be there?'

ALEKA: You shouldn't have said that.

MARO: I said 'leave, leave and I'll be there?'

FOTINI: I will discuss this no further.

ALEKA: She's right, Maro.

FOTINI: It's over.

ALEKA: What does that mean, 'Leave, leave, and I'll be there?'

MARO: I said that? I don't know ... I don't remember ... I was confused.

FOTINI: Oh, you were confused all right, because I caught you red handed.

ALEKA: You had Fatso inside.

MARO: Fatso?

FOTINI: That's why you were confused.

ALEKA: And you tell her 'Leave, leave and I'll be there'. You think she doesn't catch on when she sees Fatso's jacket in the back?

MARO: What jacket?

ALEKA: Fatso's jacket. The plaid.

MARO: Fatso's jacket?

FOTINI: Didn't I tell you she'd start doing that again?

MARO: Girls, it's not like that.

ALEKA: You've become obsessed with Fatso, Maro.

FOTINI: (*to* A) Isn't that what I told you she'd say?

MARO: (*getting angry*) Now you listen here ...

ALEKA: Face the facts Maro. You're obsessed.

MARO: And don't keep calling him Fatso. He's not at all fat.

FOTINI: He's not fat?

MARO: Is Stavros fat?

FOTINI: What is he then?

MARO: He's well built, stocky.

ALEKA: Well built, but he could stand to lose a few pounds.

MARO: He's just ample.

ALEKA: He's a little more than that really. It shows in his walk.

MARO: But he's not overweight.

FOTINI: He is overweight.

ALEKA: By the new standards he's overweight.

(*Pause.* FOTINI *paces back and forth.*)

FOTINI: Can you believe it?, I throw Anthony out and leave him suffering ... Aleka breaks the tenor's cassettes one by one ... and writes him off forever ... and here you are going against us, sticking like glue to Fatso.

MARO: If you really want to know – it wasn't Fatso.

ALEKA: It wasn't?

MARO: It wasn't.

FOTINI: Then why didn't you let me in?

MARO: Because it wasn't Fatso ... It was someone else...

ALEKA: Someone else?

FOTINI: Who was it?

MARO: I don't know ... I don't know...

ALEKA: You don't know?

MARO: Right now, I'm completely in the dark. I don't know ... Don't ask me ... There's just one thing I'll say ... He touched me and I went crazy ... His hand brushed up against me here ... and my whole body tingled!

FOTINI: You mean it wasn't Fatso?

MARO: No, Fotini, dear, it wasn't...

FOTINI: Then who was it?

MARO: Something to drink ... I need a drink...

ALEKA: Would you like a scotch?

MARO: Whatever ... He touched me and I went crazy...

ALEKA: Do you want ice?

FOTINI: So who was it?

MARO: My darling ... There I sat working on a bracelet ... And a couple walks in. A young woman and a blond man. An incredible man around thirty five. At first, nothing ... They look around ... They study the jewellery in the display windows and settle on this pin ... Anyway, I wrap the pin and he comes over to pay. So far nothing. He hands me the money ... and as I take it, a bill falls to the floor. I stoop to pick it up – he beats me to it in a flash. And just then, who knows how it happened, just like that ... Our eyes met...

ALEKA: Ohhh!

MARO: I was stunned, because he had such a profound gaze, totally unique. This deeply profound, penetrating . . . gaze . . .

ELECTRA: No shit!

MARO: Deeply penetrating.

ELECTRA: Like that commercial, where she drops her keys.

FOTINI: You mean those two were there when I arrived? When you threw me out?

MARO: Hold on dear, let me finish.

FOTINI: Because if that's who it was . . .

MARO: Hold on, darling.

ALEKA: Let her finish . . . (*She hands* MARO *a scotch.*) Here.

ELECTRA: So then what?

MARO: They leave . . . It was late. I go lock the door so I can work on the bracelet until Fotini arrives. Five minutes later the door bell rings . . . I open the door . . . And it's him . . .

ELECTRA: The incredible man!

MARO: 'Sorry,' he says, 'I forgot my cigarettes.' He closes the door behind him . . . and moves towards the back . . .

ALEKA: Was he alone?

MARO: Alone . . . But in his hand he held a yellow rose. This rose! (*Pause*) I don't know where he found this yellow rose . . .

ALEKA: How much time had passed?

MARO: Five minutes . . .

FOTINI: You don't find a rose in five minutes.

ALEKA: It just seemed like five minutes.

MARO: OK, so say it was ten minutes.

FOTINI: Unless he cut it from your garden.

MARO: I don't have yellow roses.

FOTINI: Of course you do.

MARO: Mine are white.

FOTINI: White?

ALEKA: That's right, they are.

FOTINI: Even so, in five minutes you can't get rid of a broad and find a rose.

MARO: Anyway . . . the point is he looked me deep in the eyes . . .

ELECTRA: Again?

MARO: Again. And he says ... 'Before this rose wilts I'll be back.'

ALEKA: Aaah!

FOTINI: Now you're justified.

MARO: That's why I told you to leave. Don't you see, Fotini dear? Because if...

FOTINI: You're completely justified.

ALEKA: And then? What happened after that?

MARO: Then I go back and find him in exactly the same spot ... but in the meantime he'd found his cigarettes ... With that blond, sunburnt hand ... and he held the red lighter together with his cigarettes with such strength. (*She imitates him holding out his lighter and cigarettes.*) So sensuous and moody and in the other hand, oh so lightly he held the rose!

ELECTRA: That's some combination!

MARO: Oh that combination! Meanwhile, how should I respond? I was at a loss. Because how does one respond to such intensity?

ALEKA: True.

MARO: I start to say something – he beats me to it. 'I'm flying,' he says 'to Luxembourg and then I'll be back'!

FOTINI: Luxembourg?

MARO: 'Before this rose wilts,' he says, 'I'll be back'.

ELECTRTA: Unbelievable!

ALEKA: Incredible!

MARO: Just look ... if you check my pulse right now it's a hundred and fifty.

FOTINI: Why, I could tell at a glance. You were ... You must have gone right off the deep end.

MARO: Off the deep end.

FOTINI: I could tell at a glance.

MARO: It hit me like lightning.

FOTINI: Why, I touched you and you were on fire. You were steaming.

MARO: It's the first time a man's ever affected me like that, girls. It hit me like lightning!

ALEKA: It's because you dumped Fatso. Because you made the decision.

MARO: Do you think so?

ALEKA: He saw it in your eyes. It's written in your eyes. 'I got rid of Fatso – I'm free'.

FOTINI: That's it Maro!

ALEKA: Of course. You radiated freedom.

MARO: You mean that's why he came back ... He caught that.

ALEKA: During the ten years I was married, no one even looked at me. This peculiar thing had happened to me. I had fallen into a black depression. I asked myself what's going on here: Am I finished as a woman? Through? Well, not only am I not through, but I'm still going strong. Because as soon as I got divorced, and got over the panic and despair, that's when I came into my own.

FOTINI: (*enthused*) I believe you. I believe you.

ALEKA: And I had lost weight.

MARO: I want to see him again, girls ... I want to see him again.

FOTINI: And now he's gone?

MARO: He's gone to Luxembourg. But as he left, he said, 'you'll be seeing me again soon'.

FOTINI: So what's he going to do in Luxembourg?

MARO: I have no idea...

ALEKA: What does he do?

MARO: I don't know a thing about him ... Don't ask me.

ELECTRA: He must be a pilot.

MARO: Pilot?

FOTINI: Do you think he's a pilot?

ELECTRA: Yes, I'm sure. He's a pilot.

ALEKA: Why would he be a pilot?

ELECTRA: Because his hand was sunburnt. (*To* MARO) Isn't that what you said?

MARO: It was sunburnt...

ELECTRA: Which means the man's been swimming.

MARO: He's been swimming...

ELECTRA: So when did he go swimming? It's March.

FOTINI: That's it! He's a pilot and he goes to Honolulu, the Bahamas, Miami.

ELECTRA: And he swims.

FOTINI: Just think, a pilot! I love it! Just think, Aleka ... It's going to happen to us! You'll see. It's going to happen to us.

ALEKA: Really?

FOTINI: Of course. And now with this trip coming up? We'll come back brand new.

ALEKA: (*laughs*) You can say that again.

FOTINI: Even Maki at the agency said so. 'You'll come back,' he says, 'brand new.'

ALEKA: He said that?

ELECTRA: Well then you free and rejuvenated women will be singing new songs from now on!

FOTINI: New songs!

2

A day later. Afternoon. MARO *is stringing beads to make necklaces.* FOTINI *is going through various brochures from travel agencies.*

FOTINI: (*to* A) Look here ... Buddhist monks wearing orange!

ALEKA: Mmm...

FOTINI: And it says we'll visit the splendid temples ... Wat Trimetr with its golden Buddha ... Wat Po with the reclining Buddha ... the Emperor's Palace with the Emerald Buddha...

ALEKA: All that?

FOTINI: Not to mention the landscapes ... Look, Maro ... Look at this landscape!

MARO: (*without enthusiasm*) Hm. Hhmm.

FOTINI: It's fantastic! It's driving me crazy! Look at those strange trees ... the multicolored flowers ... how exotic!

ALEKA: Just tell me one thing. Are the hotels comfortable?

FOTINI: Comfortable? Comfortable?

ALEKA: Because I'm in no mood for landscapes ... I'm a woman wounded by love.

FOTINI: Look at that. Look at the lounges ... Look at the bedrooms ... Look at that.

ALEKA: Is that where we're staying?

FOTINI: Why, don't you like it? It's luxurious.

ALEKA: Good. Because when I break up I want luxury. To relax me.

FOTINI: You'll relax there ... in Thailand ... they have a different sense of time there ... No one rushes to go anywhere.

ALEKA: Good.

FOTINI: You just lie there and your thoughts withdraw from worldly matters...

ALEKA: There. That's what I want to do. Withdraw from the world.

FOTINI: Good, then. Tomorrow I'm going to book the tickets. We leave in a week. Agreed?

ALEKA: Agreed.

FOTINI: We leave in a week ... and we disappear ... to experience those ancient civilizations at last.

MARO: Just hold it right there. What about the blond?

FOTINI: What?

MARO: How can I go to Thailand?

FOTINI: I don't get you...

MARO: Because he's going to show up any day now...

FOTINI: So?

MARO: How can I leave?

ALEKA: What do you mean how can you leave?

MARO: I can't leave, Aleka ... Because he'll come ... You think I can just leave him and go?

FOTINI: What are you trying to pull on us now?

MARO: Anyway, I am not planning to lose this one.

FOTINI: Aleka, what is she talking about?

ALEKA: How should I know?

MARO: He may turn out to be the great passion of my life.

FOTINI: The passion of your life?

MARO: Why, do you doubt it?

FOTINI: Excuse me . . . just a minute . . .

MARO: Couldn't he be?

FOTINI: Excuse me, but didn't we agree that nothing would stop us from taking this trip?

MARO: We said . . .

FOTINI: So we could get some strength, to start a new life?

MARO: Fine. I'll start mine right here. I don't need trips or anything.

FOTINI: You mean you're blowing our plans sky high?

MARO: That's the man I want. I want him and I'm going to wait for him like crazy.

FOTINI: I don't believe you . . .

(*Pause*)

ALEKA: Tell me, Maro. Are you sure he'll come?

MARO: He said he'd come.

ALEKA: He said. But will he?

MARO: He said he'd come.

(*Pause.* FOTINI *paces back and forth.*)

FOTINI: And what about me?

MARO: You? What about you?

FOTINI: With Anthony, my dear, what will happen? If we don't take this trip to Thailand, I will give in to him.

MARO: Why should you give in?

FOTINI: I'm being pressured.

ALEKA: Yes Maro. She's being pressured.

FOTINI: He started sending me chocolates again. And I have a weakness for chocolates. He knows that and he takes advantage of it. Don't laugh, Aleka. How did he get to me the last time? With the Swiss chocolates. How long can I hold out if Anthony sends a box of chocolates every day? I already sent back the first batch. But how long can I hold out? I'll send them back once, twice. The third time I'll break down and I'll eat them and once I've eaten them, it's all over for me.

MARO: Fine. Then you can go with Aleka.

FOTINI: You just stop it right there. I'll have a nervous breakdown before long.

MARO: You mean I should lose out.

FOTINI: Shut up, Maro. I'm going to break down any minute now.

(*Pause*)

ALEKA: Hold on a second, Maro ... How long will we be gone? Only fifteen days.

MARO: And just suppose that he comes back somewhat delayed and doesn't find me?

ALEKA: If he comes and doesn't find you ... he'll leave a note ...

MARO: A note? What note?

ALEKA: A slip of paper, dear ... under the door. Telephone number such and such ... call me ... I'll be waiting and so on.

MARO: And if he doesn't leave a note? I'll be left hanging.

ALEKA: Why shouldn't he leave a note?

MARO: Say it's a spur of the moment reaction and he doesn't leave a note ...

ALEKA: If he really wants you he'll leave a note.

MARO: Aleka, I just don't know what to say ... Anyway he might misinterpret my absence. Take it to mean something else.

ALEKA: Such as?

MARO: Flight ... Or he might think that it was something unimportant to me ... A puff of smoke and it's gone ...

ALEKA: ...

MARO: Can you take the responsibility for something like that?

FOTINI: I don't believe it ... I'm going crazy! Just the thought of going back to Anthony drives me crazy!

MARO: If Anthony can get to you, then Fatso can get to me.

FOTINI: What do you mean? That's over, finished.

MARO: I'm not sure ...

ALEKA: Hold on a second ... Weren't you crying and carrying on when he knocked his wife up?

MARO: ...

ALEKA: Didn't you tell us the whole sad story? Give us a

blow by blow account? I ate all the pistachios to calm my nerves! Because of you I ate a pound of pistachios.

MARO: Yes, but he said she'd got an abortion.

FOTINI: (*furious*) Look dear, did he or did he not knock her up?

MARO: Yes, but since the abortion I'm vulnerable.

FOTINI: Aleka? I'm going crazy!

ALEKA: So why get upset? Let her go back to Fatso and take up when she left off. What's it to you?

MARO: That's just the problem Aleka ... I can't stand waiting around in the shadows any more ... I want him to take me out to the theater, to a movie ... a restaurant ... Nothing. Unless he gets to build a summer home somewhere so I can at least go swimming with him ... but where do I end up going? To Levanates. You saw what I went through all last summer.

ALEKA: That's true ... it was a disaster...

MARO: Only old women and children ... these miserable people on a dirty beach...

ALEKA: And he's a lousy architect as well...

MARO: Do you see what I mean?

ALEKA: You should have dumped him when he knocked his wife up the first time. You made your mistake then. You kept him. You sealed your fate.

MARO: Well now I want to escape that fate. I want to grab hold of the blond and escape. And you put a knife to my throat.

FOTINI: Aleka, be careful. Just watch what you say. She's trying to put the blame on us. That's exactly what Anthony does. He makes me feel guilty for supposedly pushing him away.

MARO: I want to be free! I want to be free!

ALEKA: Wait a minute, Maro...

(MARO *is taking tissues out of her bag.*)

ALEKA: When did he say he'd show?

MARO: He said before the rose wilts...

ALEKA: Fine ... When do we leave for Thailand? A week

from now. Within one week we'll know. Will he, won't he?

MARO: Aleka...

ALEKA: What's all the fuss about? How long do roses last anyway? Three or four days.

MARO: Yes, but something might happen to him. Something might come up. Shouldn't he have some leeway?

ALEKA: OK, let's give him some leeway. Let's change the water. (*She takes the vase and goes to empty the water.*) I'll give it a little aspirin ... and it will last longer. But if he doesn't show up and the rose wilts, we book tickets and leave for Thailand.

FOTINI: Aleka, what's come over you? What a lukewarm stance!

ALEKA: What can we do? You see a woman suffering ... she's in love ... What can we do?

FOTINI: And how long exactly did it take her to fall in love? One minute? One minute?

ALEKA: One minute.

FOTINI: It's bullshit!

ALEKA: You see, Fatso's a big part of the problem here. Do you understand? What else can we do? There, the rose is ready ... (*She sets the rose on the table.*)

3

Five days later. It's four in the morning. ALEKA *and* MARO *are eating cake. The yellow rose in the vase is wilted.*

MARO: The icing's nice. It has cherries in it. (*Pause*) Anyway, I'm through with Fatso I've had enough.

ALEKA: Enough's enough.

MARO: Years now. (*Pause*) And there's something else I've discovered. He lied to me about his wife having the abortion.

ALEKA: (*her mouth full*) Oh, the bastard!

MARO: That's right ... She didn't have an abortion after all, Aleka. Here, have this piece with the plum. It's good.

(*Pause*)

MARO: And what if he calls?

ALEKA: What if who calls?

MARO: Stefano. Would you talk to him?

ALEKA: What are you talking about?

MARO: If he calls? Would you talk to him?

ALEKA: He won't call. He didn't call me on my birthday.

MARO: Just say, if he calls ... if the telephone suddenly rings and it's Stefano.

ALEKA: He's not going to call ... It's over.

MARO: You think so?

ALEKA: It's over, Maro. It's over ... Now let's just go on our trip ... take in a movie ... smoke a cigarette. Things like that.

(*Pause*)

MARO: May I ask you something? Are you all that up for it? Is it so all important we leave for Thailand?

ALEKA: Well, we've scheduled it.

MARO: Yes, but what I mean is, do we simply have to go to Thailand?

ALEKA: Maro, he didn't show, it's over. What are you going to do? Wait a lifetime? That's not the way things work. He didn't show, it's over.

MARO: But in life things are relative so to speak ... They look that way but they're not that way ... And anything ... time ... circumstances ... the unexpected ... can play a big part.

ALEKA: What are you saying? Do you realize what you're saying?

MARO: And what harm would it do, say, if instead of leaving now ... we left, let's say, in a month?

ALEKA: We can't put it off a month. I have to take out the summer stock ... I have the display windows to do...

MARO: Oh, really?

ALEKA: And anyway, what would we do with Fotini? She's set her heart on it now. The rose wilted ... it's over. She's arranged it with the bank – taken her leave and so forth...

MARO: But...

ALEKA: No more delays. And I'm warning you, don't you dare mention it to her – all hell will break loose.

MARO: What got into her? What does she want? Why is she so set on this trip?

ALEKA: Well, why are you so stuck on this guy?

MARO: I was affected by the event, Aleka. The fact that everything happened so fast. The tension ... the atmosphere...

ALEKA: What atmosphere? You weren't with him more than two minutes ... And he was with someone else.

MARO: (laughs) So he was!

ALEKA: What's got into you?

MARO: I don't know. What can I say? I think of him constantly ... It's him, only him, constantly...

ALEKA: (laughing) You've made your point.

MARO: The phone rings and I jump up ... I say there he is! It's him! That's him! And I run smack into Fatso.

ALEKA: There's that too.

MARO: And as the days pass his face fades from my memory ... And that tears me up ... It's really getting on my nerves.

ALEKA: Yes, but control yourself girl.

MARO: Control, Aleka, is for separations ... I can't control myself through first encounters.

ALEKA: So what happens now? You're going to hang by the phone forever? Don't you see what the phone did to me?

MARO: When you waited and he never called. How terrible!

ALEKA: When I don't know if he called.

MARO: On your birthday?

ALEKA: That's what been tearing me apart these past ten days. Not knowing what happened ... Because at twelve o'clock sharp ... at twelve o'clock which was the crucial hour ... Electra gets on the phone.

MARO: Aaaa!

ALEKA: I wanted ... to choke her. Because she knew that at twelve midnight Stefano and I always opened a bottle of champagne ... Well, at two minutes to twelve Electra gets on the phone.

MARO: Oh no...

ALEKA: So I say to her. 'OK now get off the phone'. And what do you think she says? 'Why, you got a problem?'

MARO: You're kidding!

ALEKA: She did it on purpose.

MARO: She could have forgotten.

ALEKA: Who forgot? What are you talking about? Electra? Given the hatred that she feels for Stefano...

MARO: You've got a point there.

ALEKA: For her to get on the phone at twelve o'clock? Two minutes to twelve? And she stayed on, the devil ... a half hour to the minute. I paced back and forth ... back and forth ... She didn't bat an eyelash. 'So what else is new, Jason' and 'What's playing at the Danaos on Monday?' Well, I took three of those three milligram pills. The pink ones.

MARO: That was murder.

ALEKA: That was murder all right. Because I keep thinking that if Stefanos was at that moment in Germany in the rain and the snow alone ... desperate ... with a telephone in front of him ... and he says 'I can't stand it any more. I'll call her' And he calls ... and it's busy. For an hour!

MARO: Oh, isn't that awful?

ALEKA: Do you understand what that little bitch did to me? She poisoned my soul with uncertainty.

MARO: Of course ... You're right ... Because he might have called.

ALEKA: And just listen to this. When Electra hung up ... She finished her conversation and hung up ... and the minute the receiver's down I hear it ring twice ... Like something's left over...

MARO: What?

ALEKA: A ring left over ... Like it was, say, the last signal from Stefano in Germany...

MARO: How do you mean?

ALEKA: My dear, he called ... and got a busy signal ... in the meantime Electra hung up ... before he did ... Right?

MARO: Hmm...

ALEKA: And this last ring of his was left over ... Right? Don't you see, the instant he lowers the receiver to hang up ... That ring was left over.

MARO: Oh I get it.

ALEKA: And afterwards ... silence.

MARO: I see...

ALEKA: I haven't slept a wink since that night.

MARO: The uncertainty ... How awful!

ALEKA: It's been ten days since I last slept.

MARO: And did you know that insomnia makes you crave sugar?

ALEKA: I know, I know ... Luckily I went out onto the balcony to get some air and saw your light on ... You weren't asleep either...

MARO: How could I sleep? I go to bed – but I can't sleep.

ALEKA: I know, it's awful. Me too ... I close my eyes ... and nothing happens ... and it's always Delos ... That summer in Delos ... when Stefano and I got lost among the statues...

MARO: (*eating*) Yes...

ALEKA: We missed the last boat and the sun went down ... that sunset ... and the wind blew my hat away ... That picture keeps coming back to me ... The straw hat with the bouquet of violets circling through the air, disappearing into the sea. That picture. And Stefano singing...

MARO: What happened? Did you spend the night there? I don't remember...

ALEKA: No dear ... People on a yacht heard him singing and sailed in close to shore. They were shipowners ... industrialists, something like that.

MARO: They followed his voice?

ALEKA: What a voice! See what a little bastard he is? He defeated the waves, the wind, everything! We saw them suddenly on shore. That was really something! And then there were torrents of praise and laughter ... Because his pants fell down.

MARO: Ha ha ha!

ALEKA: Ha ha ... Haven't I told you?

(MARO *laughs.*)

ALEKA: We had made love ... He hadn't buttoned up properly ... He didn't have time ... He heard voices and went a bit too fast...

MARO: And his pants fell off ... (*Laughs*)

ALEKA: Unforgettable moments...

MARO: Yes, they are unforgettable.

ALEKA: Those unforgettable events, Maro dear, torture me ... (*Lights a cigarette*)

MARO: Give me one ... (*Takes it*) Today I have smoked my head off...

ALEKA: And the whole trip back to Mykonos on the yacht was a musical delirium ... Stefano sang Italian boating songs ... then Russian ... then Zakinthian. '*Venite al l'agile barchetta mia, Santa Lucia, Santa Lucia.*' (*She suddenly bursts into tears.*) I can't bear it ... I just can't bear it, Maro...

MARO: How did things turn out this way?

ALEKA: I miss him, Maro...

MARO: I know you do...

ALEKA: I miss him so much...

MARO: Come on now, take it easy.

ALEKA: Yes...

MARO: Calm down ... (*Embraces her*)

ALEKA: I don't want to wake Electra.

MARO: Shall I get you something to drink? (*Pause*) Do you have anything in the fridge? (*Goes to the refrigerator*)

ALEKA: (*crying softly*) Was that it then? Was that all and it's over?

MARO: That Maestro is to blame, Aleka dear ... That foul mouthed Patriarcheas.

ALEKA: He's the one...

MARO: But then there's Stefano, my dear. He's far too rigid.

ALEKA: Aaah!

MARO: No sense of humour. (*Gives her orange juice*) Because to tell you the truth, what Patriarcheas said wasn't so terrible.

ALEKA: Are you kidding? It wasn't terrible that he said I

have a beautiful ass? The most beautiful ass?

MARO: Well, they say those things in artistic circles.

ALEKA: Aaah, that Maestro ... He's the one ... He ruined everything.

MARO: No sense of humor. That's it.

ALEKA: The misery in my life began with him ... and who knows how long it will last...

4

A day later. Afternoon.

ALEKA: Anthony?

FOTINI: The bastard tried to kill me. He tried to kill me ... I still haven't recovered. I'm shaking like a leaf ... I'm going to pieces.

ALEKA: Will you tell us what happened?

FOTINI: I need a minute to recover ... just a minute ... Because I'm not well.

ALEKA: Do you want a brandy?

FOTINI: Yes, yes, ... some brandy.

(ALEKA *pours a brandy*.)

ALEKA: To calm you.

FOTINI: Good. Give me some brandy.

ELECTRA: A real incident, eh?

FOTINI: He was waiting for me ... outside the bank.

ALEKA: No shit!

FOTINI: Lying in wait ... I say 'What are you doing here?' 'Nothing' he says ... 'Let me take you to Lycabettus for our last dinner together.'

ALEKA: And you went?

FOTINI: I went ... I thought, he deserves one last dinner ... Everyone deserves one last dinner ... How can you refuse someone a last dinner?

ELECTRA: So what did you eat?

FOTINI: What did I eat? Did I get a chance to eat?

ELECTRA: Why?

FOTINI: Because as we were being served ... I had ordered steak with mushrooms which I really like ...

ELECTRA: So do I.

FOTINI: He asks me, 'Why don't you want us to get married?' I say, 'And live a whole lifetime together?' 'Yes,' he says. 'A whole lifetime together.' I say 'That's not possible'. He says 'Why not?' I say 'Better let it go' ... and I started to eat my steak. And he says 'No, I want to know the truth. I want to know the truth.' 'You want to know the truth?' I ask him. 'I want to know the truth,' he says. At which point I see red and I let him have it. 'Because you're flat'.

MARO: Aaaaah!

ALEKA: You said that?

FOTINI: I said it! 'You're flat. My life with you is of no interest whatsoever'.

ELECTRA: Oh, fuck!

FOTINI: Well, he asked for it. 'Let's get married. Let's get married Let's get married.' Look you, I don't wanna get married.

ALEKA: That must have hit him like a ton of bricks.

FOTINI: Exactly ... 'How's that?' he says, 'What? Say that again' ... I say 'Flat' and go to cut my steak. Well, that's when I see my plate moving away from me.

MARO: Moving away from you?

FOTINI: The plate along with everything else on the table started moving away.

ELECTRA: How do you mean?

FOTINI: Slowly ... He was pulling the tablecloth ... And suddenly he says. 'You mean, I'm flat!' And with one jerk he sends everything flying.

MARO: Aaah!

ALEKA: Aaah!

FOTINI: And the moment everything went flying something terrible happened. I caught this glint in his eye. Knives ... guns ... all the weapons at that moment in his eye ... That's when my knees gave out. I don't know how I

found the courage to get up and run out! Luckily a cab
was passing. I grabbed it and left.

ALEKA: Unbelievable!

FOTINI: I was paralyzed ... stunned. I thought to myself,
'Now he's going to kill me!'

ELECTRA: A real incident, hey?

FOTINI: Luckily the cab came by.

ALEKA: I wouldn't have thought, you know, that he'd react
like that ...

FOTINI: Now do you see?

ELECTRA: He played it tough ...

ALEKA: Well done, Anthony! Did you expect that from him?

ELECTRA: Anthony's great. (*She laughs.*)

FOTINI: You're laughing?

ALEKA: (*laughs*) Anthony's showing his teeth.

FOTINI: I'm telling you he almost killed me, and you laugh?

MARO: Tell me, was that it?

FOTINI: What?

MARO: Was that all the killing he tried to do? You saw
swords and knives in his eyes?

FOTINI: I'm not getting your point.

MARO: That was all there was to it? And you're leading us
on all this time, playing up the suspense, turning it into a
thriller?

FOTINI: I saw it in his eyes, Maro ...

MARO: (*sarcastic*) Sure ...

FOTINI: He tried to kill me.

MARO: Bullshit.

FOTINI: Listen girl, did you see his eyes? You did not see
his eyes when he was holding the knife ...

MARO: What knife?

ELECTRA: He pulled a knife?

FOTINI: The cheese knife!

ALEKA: The cheese knife?

FOTINI: Of course. When he pulled the tablecloth ... the
instant everything went flying through the air ... the
cheese knife passed in front of him. He makes a lightning-
quick move and grabs it.

ELECTRA: Aaaah!

FOTINI: He holds it briefly . . . like this . . . for seconds. And then he lets it fall to the floor. That lunge in the air for the knife and that hold – paralyzed me . . .

MARO: . . .

FOTINI: That's what I'm talking about, Maro dear. Do you understand?

MARO: I haven't understood anything.

FOTINI: There she goes again!

MARO: Anthony is a calm man.

ELECTRA: Maro, you're being irrelevant.

MARO: Calm and gentle.

ELECTRA: It's the calm ones you should fear. Calm people perpetrate the biggest crimes.

FOTINI: There you are! Do you hear that?

ELECTRA: And don't be fooled when things look calm. Because just when things seem calm . . . bam bam bam and your picture's on the news.

FOTINI: Hear that? The bastard's gonna waste me.

ALEKA: Electra, what was that all about?

FOTINI: I'll die a victim . . . You'll see. You'll find me in some bushes . . . and they'll broadcast the police investigation . . .

ALEKA: What was that all about?

MARO: Electra's fantasies . . . (*She takes her salad and starts eating.*)

ELECTRA: Don't take it so lightly. Because they could find her in a ditch.

FOTINI: A threat has been made on my life now, Aleka, do you understand?

ELECTRA: Anyway, whatever happens we'll go as witnesses. We'll say he threatened her. Let the bastard rot in jail.

ALEKA: Electra, cut out the jokes.

ELECTRA: I'm not joking, Mom. He showed signs of aggression. Agreed?

FOTINI: He showed signs of aggression.

ELECTRA: For the first time.

FOTINI: For the first time.

ELECTRA: Well, that's what's dangerous. The first time.

FOTINI: That's what scares me, Electra.

MARO: Yeah, yeah ... Swords and knives ... (*She laughs.*)

ELECTRA: And now that you mention it, he could be after you this very minute.

FOTINI: Aaah!

ELECTRA: Tell me, does he know you're here?

FOTINI: No ... He stayed with the waiters to clean up the mess.

ELECTRA: He'll suspect you are ... Let me pull these drapes.

FOTINI: Yes, yes. Pull the drapes.

ELECTRA: Just to be sure.

FOTINI: Pull the drapes.

ALEKA: Do you think he'd dare come here?

MARO: (*to A*) Eat your salad, dear. Don't mind them. They're delirious.

ALEKA: (*takes her salad and eats*) He wouldn't dare come. After what he did to me?

FOTINI: Oh, yes he would.

ALEKA: Snoring at the opera while Stefano was singing? How could he dare come here?

ELECTRA: He would dare because now he's wild with rage.

ALEKA: Do you think so?

FOTINI: Electra, look out the window. He may hiding somewhere.

ELECTRA: I looked. No one's there.

FOTINI: No one was there a minute ago. Now he could be.

ELECTRA: Right. (*She goes and looks.*)

FOTINI: Do you know what a bastard he is? He shows up out of nowhere.

ELECTRA: There's no one there.

ALEKA: So he's wild with rage?

ELECTRA: Of course.

ALEKA: Do you really think so?

ELECTRA: Definitely.

ALEKA: And what do you know about these things?

ELECTRA: I read the newspapers and draw conclusions.

FOTINI: He'll kill me ... He'll catch me turning a corner ... on a side street ... who knows ... He'll kill me ...

How can I go out? How can I go home tonight?

ALEKA: Why go? You don't have to go anywhere.

FOTINI: I'm scared Aleka...

ALEKA: You're staying here. You'll sleep here.

FOTINI: I'm scared. (*She cries.*)

ALEKA: And no one will find you. (*A small pause*) I can't believe this happened. (*She embraces* FOTINI *and soothes her.*) Come on now, that's it. Don't be frightened. Drink a little brandy...

(FOTINI *drinks.*)

ALEKA: We'll call the bank tomorrow to say you're sick and you'll stay here ... we'll sleep together...

FOTINI: I'll stay here.

ALEKA: I'll give you freshly ironed pajamas and I have an extra toothbrush for you ... And slippers...

FOTINI: The toothbrush I left last summer?

ALEKA: I'll get you a new one. Don't worry.

FOTINI: I'll stay here...

ALEKA: Yes, my baby ... You'll stay here.

ELECTRA: The important thing is to get through this crucial phase. If you can get through this phase then the rage subsides.

FOTINI: Do you think so?

ELECTRA: But in order for his rage to subside you have to go to Thailand.

FOTINI: Yes, yes, let's go.

ELECTRA: As soon as possible. While there's still time.

MARO: Say, don't you have a class to go to?

ELECTRA: Until he calms down some...

FOTINI: So he'll lose track of me...

ELECTRA: Because, otherwise, the crisis won't pass.

FOTINI: And accept the fact and say: 'She doesn't belong to me any more'...

ELECTRA: That's it.

FOTINI: (*to* A) And if he came here, you wouldn't let him in. Would you Aleka?

ALEKA: Me let him in? You think I'm crazy?

FOTINI: Because he'll ask you. He'll plead with you. He'll fall to his knees. He'll say he's dying, wasting away, his life's running out . . . But you'll resist. You won't give in . . .

ALEKA: Don't worry.

FOTINI: You won't give in no matter what.

ALEKA: No matter what.

FOTINI: Because he'll try to break you.

ALEKA: No way . . .

FOTINI: Yeah, no way, but the last time we had a fight he came here and sat down to a spaghetti dinner.

ALEKA: That was different . . .

FOTINI: Because now my life's in danger . . .

MARO: Oh, stop for goodness sake!

FOTINI: He'll kill me . . .

MARO: Just stop this whole farce.

FOTINI: After what I did to him, he'll kill me, that's all there is to it.

MARO: You're hysterical. 'He'll kill me, he'll kill me.' You're driving me crazy. He'll kill you . . . Who's going to kill you? Anthony?

FOTINI: You've no reason to talk. The rose wilted. Didn't it wilt? It's over. Don't say another word. We gave you more leeway and everything. Now it's over. Now it's my turn. We're leaving for Thailand. Because there's a limit. I've had enough! The blond, the blond, the blond . . .

MARO: I can't take this any more . . . Where are my keys?

FOTINI: And give Aleka money to go buy the tickets tomorrow. Because I, of course, will not leave this place. I will leave here only to catch that plane.

MARO: Where did I put those keys, Aleka?

FOTINI: I will leave here only to catch that plane.

MARO: (*to* F) I can't stand you any more . . .

FOTINI: Right Aleka?

ALEKA: Yes, my baby . . .

MARO: And you, Aleka, are wrong to encourage her.

ALEKA: I beg your pardon . . .

MARO: Instead of coming to her senses and cutting the crap . . .

ALEKA: What crap? Just the other day weren't you insisting he's a coarse vulgar doctor?

MARO: But Anthony has, in fact, made some highly sensitive moves.

FOTINI: Aaah...

MARO: Why, isn't it true?

ALEKA: Hold it right there, Maro...

MARO: And he adores her.

FOTINI: She's trying to trick me into going back to him.

ALEKA: Three days ago you had a different opinion...

FOTINI: She's doing this because of the blond, Aleka. She's willing to sacrifice me for the blond!

MARO: Oh, get off it, Fotini. I just can't stand you any longer ... But this is what you usually do, and you'll probably end up without a man at all. It's typical of you.

FOTINI: She wants to send me back to my murderer. Don't you see?

MARO: I can't stand you and all your exaggerations any more.

FOTINI: Back to my murderer ... (*She cries.*)

MARO: What did I do with my keys?

FOTINI: Do you see, Aleka?

MARO: You blow everything totally out of proportion.

ELECTRA: Your keys are there ... On the mantle.

MARO: And then you get us involved. Like that other time you told us, 'That man's looking at us ... Look, that man's watching us' ... Do you remember that incident?

FOTINI: Which one?

MARO: At the cinema ... the Boboniera...

FOTINI: When?

MARO: When that man was sitting there waiting for the film to start ... and suddenly you say, 'Look at that man, I think he's watching us ... he's watching us. It's weird the way he's watching us. Who's that weird man who's watching us'...

ALEKA: Really, that was something! (*She laughs.*)

MARO: (*to* E) Meanwhile, with all this watching going on, this man starts wondering why we're watching him. And he starts watching us. Looking to see if we're watching him ... And Fotini says, 'See, what did I tell you? He's watching us.'

ELECTRA: Did that really happen?

MARO: Last summer ...

(*They start laughing more and more out of control.*)

ALEKA: With this totally unsuspecting person.

MARO: This little man ... This fat little man who was taken by surprise ...

ELECTRA: You guys, I don't believe this!

MARO: And when the film was over ... we fell over ourselves trying to get out of there in case he tried to follow us ...

ALEKA: And we stepped all over people getting out ...

(*The laughter peaks.*)

ELECTRA: Ha ha haaaa!

ALEKA: And we made fools of ourselves ... And she's screaming (*meaning* FOTINI) 'Faster! Faster!'

MARO: We were running like madwomen to get to the car ...

ELECTRA: This is killing me ...

MARO: ... so he wouldn't follow us ...

ALEKA: (*doubled up with laughter*) Stop, Maro!

MARO: (*pointing to* A) ... and she loses the keys ...

(FOTINI *is carried along and laughs too.*)

MARO: And we see him come out ...

ALEKA: Oblivious ...

MARO: ... and turn the corner ... and disappear ...

ELECTRA: Ha ha ha ...

FOTINI: And we were left looking for the keys ...

ALEKA: And just you try finding keys in the dark ...

FOTINI: We spent half an hour looking for those keys ...

5

Two days later. Noon.

ELECTRA *and* FOTINI *are working out. Music on the stereo.*

ELECTRA: OK, again ... Let's go.

FOTINI: I can't do any more. I'm hungry ... Do you think she'll at least bring some food or will she forget?

ELECTRA: She will, don't worry. She never forgets food.

FOTINI: So can you tell me what's taking her so long?

ELECTRA: Don't you know my mother? She always loses track of time. She'll be here.

FOTINI: I'm starving!

ELECTRA: I'll play you something really nice now ... (*Goes and changes the cassette*)

FOTINI: So tell me ... Will you paint the walls?

ELECTRA: Of course. This will be all painted over ... You won't recognize it.

FOTINI: I won't, hey?

ELECTRA: Of course not ... After all it's going to be a hide-out for anarchists.

FOTINI: Really!

ELECTRA: Green ... And from here on up ... black.

FOTINI: Black?

ELECTRA: Black with graffiti ... political slogans ...

FOTINI: Really! Your mother will have a fit.

ELECTRA: You can say that again ... (*They laugh.*)

FOTINI: But you'll be playing the lead role.

ELECTRA: Of course.

FOTINI: As long as Maro's blond doesn't suddenly appear because then ...

ELECTRA: Don't worry.about that.

FOTINI: How can I not worry? She's lovesick! She jumps on her emotions and rides away ...

ELECTRA: Don't worry.

FOTINI: Don't you see how she avoids bringing the money so we can buy our tickets? She's waiting for him.

ELECTRA: Don't worry. He, at any rate, is not about to show. You've got my word on that.

FOTINI: How can you know that?

ELECTRA: From the way she told us he held the lighter. (*She demonstrates.*) Turned outwards ... Isn't that how he held it?

FOTINI: Yeah, turned outwards.

ELECTRA: Well, the ones who hold a lighter like that don't come back. They disappear.

FOTINI: No kidding?

ELECTRA: It's a fact.

FOTINI: You mean there's no way he'll show up?

ELECTRA: Look, you have my word for it ... It's over.

FOTINI: Great! You just gave me strength. Just now you gave me strength.

(ALEKA *enters with a heightened air of exhaustion. She collapses on the couch.*)

ALEKA: (*absently*) Electra, dear, make me a cup of coffee.

(ELECTRA *watches her with surprise.*)

ALEKA: Make your mommy some coffee...

FOTINI: What's the matter, Aleka?

ALEKA: (*at a loss*) Ah Fotini, my dear Fotini ...

FOTINI: Are you all right?

ALEKA: Fotini dear ... How things turn out sometimes...

FOTINI: Why, what happened?

ALEKA: How could I have known when I left the house this morning, what state I would find myself in at this moment ... Not knowing where I am, which way is up ... what I will do tomorrow ... what I will do the day after tomorrow ... what I will do the next moment...

FOTINI: Aleka, what are you talking about?

ALEKA: You sit down and you plan things ... You say: I'll do this ... I'll do that...

(ELECTRA *brings coffee.*)

ALEKA: Nonsense! Life comes along like a huge wave and blasts your plans ... your emotions ... belies all your expectations. And you? A victim ... A victim of life...

FOTINI: (*to E*) What is she talking about?

ELECTRA: How should I know.

Aleka: And you're swept away by this wave . . . and it takes you away . . . and away . . . and away . . . You resist. I don't want this, you say . . . But life doesn't take you into account at all . . . It says, 'You go, whether you want to or not' . . .

ELECTRA: Mom, what has happened to you? Are you delirious?

ALEKA: I'm delirious . . . I'm in a state of delirium.

ELECTRA: Here . . . have some coffee.

ALEKA: Because where did I find myself today? Where did the wave take me?

FOTINI: Where did it take you, Aleka, dear?

ALEKA: To the hospital.

ELECTRA: To the hospital?

FOTINI: Good God!

ELECTRA: Were you in an accident?

ALEKA: Did I ever imagine myself closing the shop at a moment's notice only to end up at the hospital?

FOTINI: For chrissake, talk, girl. Tell us what happened.

ALEKA: Aah . . . it happened at Malakassa . . .

ELECTRA: At Malakassa?

ALEKA: Don't ask me for details . . . I don't know . . . supposedly they found him in the opposite lane . . .

ELECTRA: Who?

ALEKA: How did he land in the opposite lane? I can't understand that.

FOTINI: Who, Aleka dear, who?

ALEKA: Unless he had things on his mind . . . if he was thinking about things . . . (*She drinks coffee.*) Because Stefano learned to drive in Germany . . .

ELECTRA: Stefano?

FOTINI: Stefano came back?

ELECTRA: Oh shit. Fuck!

ALEKA: German drivers are the best in Europe. They don't come any better. The cab drivers for instance. The best cab drivers have all worked in Germany.

FOTINI: Forget the cab drivers of Germany. We know about them. Tell us what happened.

ALEKA: ... Severe hemorrhage.

FOTINI: Well, did they stop it?

ALEKA: Seven doctors over him ... seven doctors and eight nurses...

FOTINI: Because if they stopped it...

ALEKA: They stopped it.

FOTINI: Well, if they stopped it, it's over. Those hemorrhages as soon as they stop, it's over. Do you understand, Electra? There's no danger of him, say ... The thing is to stop the hemorrhage. The hemorrhaging stops? It's over. He lives.

ALEKA: He lives, but how does he live? A broken leg, an broken arm ... and one or two ribs...

ELECTRA: Oh, well then it's nothing.

ALEKA: What do you mean nothing?

ELECTRA: What I mean is, he's alive.

(*Pause.* ALEKA *drinks coffee.*)

ALEKA: Fotini, did you expect Stefano to return?

FOTINI: ...

ALEKA: Suddenly, like that?

FOTINI: ...

ALEKA: Did you expect that?

FOTINI: So now what?

ALEKA: But Fotini, dear ... the state I found him in ... Unbelievable conditions ... Inexcusable. I walk into a ward for ten ... I mean, what can I say? Together with the riffraff. They didn't recognize him. You see?

FOTINI: I see...

ALEKA: That's the disadvantage that opera singers have. They're not recognized by the uninitiated.

FOTINI: I see.

ALEKA: At any rate, to tell the truth ... When someone has personality ... He was stunning.

FOTINI: Who, Stefano?

ALEKA: He was stunning. Asleep ... sedated ... and his personality shone! Was it his beard? ... was it his curly hair, his beautiful curls? ... was it his colouring? ... what can I say? He absolutely shone! He's got that dark blond colouring see?

FOTINI: So?

ALEKA: Well that man was just thrown into a ward with ten other people. I was furious. Furious. So I said, 'Don't you recognize him? Don't you see that this man is not a common person?' Then there's this silence ... they exchange glances ... and before you know it ... they ring some bells ... these nurses close in on me ... whispers and buzzing and this little doctor arrives like a keynote speaker. He gives his speech and then the head doctor arrives, the Professor. And the Professor addresses me. He asks me, 'What is your relationship to him?' Now what should I tell him? What can I say Fotini dear, when he asks 'What are you to him'? Can you tell the story of a lifetime in one word?

ELECTRA: What lifetime? It was three years.

ALEKA: Anyway...

FOTINI: I understand.

ALEKA: Do you, Fotini?

FOTINI: You gave in. Don't tell me you gave in, because I'll go mad. Did you give in?

ALEKA: No, Fotini, my dear, I did not give in.

FOTINI: What did he say to you? Did he say anything?

ALEKA: He couldn't say anything. He wasn't quite awake yet.

FOTINI: Good. You did well to leave before he woke up. Good for you.

ALEKA: Yes, but I have to go back again.

FOTINI: You're going back?

ELECTRA: Shit. Fuck.

ALEKA: Because the nurse says to me, 'Why don't you go bring him some pyjamas?' I say, 'His?' She says, 'It's better if they're his.'

FOTINI: That's it ... You're ready to give in...

ALEKA: No, Fotini dear...

FOTINI: He'll see you, he'll look into your eyes, he'll call you Alekoushka ... and it's all over. You'll give in. No way. You're not going anywhere.

ALEKA: And what about the reporters?

FOTINI: What reporters?

ALEKA: Don't you know they're waiting to get to him? Do you want them to photograph him in a ward with ten people? I have to get him into a private room.

ELECTRA: Yeah, the reporters are shitting all over themselves for Stefano.

ALEKA: Listen to her . . . Such vulgarity! I mean, really!

ELECTRA: Oh, lay off . . . (*She lies on the sofa, takes a magazine and leafs through it.*)

FOTINI: Let his niece find him a room.

ALEKA: Who, Christine? She's incapable. (*Pause*) And at some point, Electra, you must learn that we are, after all, human beings.

ELECTRA: . . .

ALEKA: Do you understand?

(ELECTRA *doesn't answer.*)

ALEKA: Life is not only being in love. There are human factors to be considered as well.

FOTINI: So tell me, how long will this take?

ALEKA: What?

FOTINI: These 'human factors,' how long will they take?

ALEKA: Everything's so uncertain. Who knows how things will go. There might be complications. I must be by his side.

FOTINI: And how long will it take for you to be by his side?

ALEKA: It might take a week . . .

FOTINI: A week?

ALEKA: It might take a month . . .

FOTINI: A month?

ALEKA: Who will take care of him?

FOTINI: And what about Thailand?

ALEKA: And then there are the artichokes.

FOTINI: Artichokes?

ALEKA: Oh, my God! Thank goodness I thought of it! He's allergic to artichokes. Will he remember to tell them that when he wakes up? If they serve him artichokes what happens? Oh, my God! I have to leave, I have to leave and get his things. Let's see now, his bathrobe ... his pyjamas ... his cologne...

FOTINI: Electra, what's happening?

ELECTRA: What's happening, Fotini? Don't you see what's happening?

ALEKA: Pictures, for the reporters ... and I'm gone.

(ALEKA *goes upstairs. Suddenly* ELECTRA *throws the magazine aside, gets on the bicycle and starts pedalling to let off steam.*)

FOTINI: (*for* ALEKA *to hear*) Listen here, you ... His hemorrhaging stopped, he's out of the woods. But me, whose life is in danger, who's going to save me? (*Pause*) Because I'm warning you. If we don't leave as soon as possible, you're in for a big shock. Because Anthony will kill me. (*Pause*) I'm telling you, he'll kill me. And you'll discover me any day now lying in a pool of blood ... (*She cries.*)

ALEKA: (*from the top of the stairs*) By the way, Electra, what's happened to Stefano's clothes? The suitcase with Stefano's clothes which I put up over the closet.

ELECTRA: After all this time you want Stefano's clothes?

ALEKA: Look kid, I want Stefano's clothes.

ELECTRA: They no longer exist. I threw them out.

ALEKA: (*coming downstairs*) You what?

FOTINI: Good for you!

ALEKA: You threw out Stefano's clothes?

ELECTRA: Weren't you the one who said, 'Throw them out?'

ALEKA: I said that?

ELECTRA: That night he left you. When he called you a whore, took the car and left for Germany.

ALEKA: Oh, my God! You threw out Stefano's clothes?

FOTINI: Good for her. He walked out, his things should leave too.

ALEKA: I'll go mad...

ELECTRA: Didn't you say you didn't want to see them? Not his clothes, nor his photographs?

ALEKA: You threw out the photographs too?

ELECTRA: The whole suitcase. The garbage truck took it.

ALEKA: But those photographs were a part of my life ... The best moments I ever had with Stefano were in them. Our best moments ... You threw away those photographs?

ELECTRA: Weren't you shouting, 'I'm going to throw them away and never see them again?' Well, I threw them away for you.

ALEKA: Never mind what I said. It was a passing moment. A rage, a despair...

ELECTRA: I don't know about that.

ALEKA: I had a photograph with my hair dyed red ... We had it taken on Andros ... at Anerousa. (*Suddenly*) Did you really throw them away? Are you telling me the truth – you threw them away?

(ELECTRA *pedals furiously.*)

ALEKA: It's not possible. You've hidden them somewhere.

(ELECTRA *pedals.*)

ALEKA: You stop that pedalling this instant.

ELECTRA: (*stops suddenly*) I threw them out.

ALEKA: What right do you have to throw away my life?

ELECTRA: Mom, lay off the melodrama.

ALEKA: What right do you have, you monster? What right?

ELECTRA: I have the right ever since that night you were beside yourself with despair ... And you kept saying 'I see crazy clouds swirling inside me and they're bringing the storm' ... And there I was, confused, and I didn't know what to do ... That's what right I have.

ALEKA: I said those things?

ELECTRA: For him. For that fucking asshole.

ALEKA: It seems I was having a crisis ... But that's all over now, Electra, dear...

ELEKTRA: What's over?

ALEKA: It's in the past now.

ELECTRA: You're getting ready to drag him back in here again.

ALEKA: Don't worry, he wont come ... He won't come.

ELECTRA: I am warning you, though. I'm prepared to go to extremes, Fotini, you're a witness.

FOTINI: I believe you.

ELECTRA: If you so much as make a move, my mind's made up. I'll go to that hospital and tear the place apart.

ALEKA: You'll go where?

ELECTRA: Go through that door, and you'll see what's in store for you.

FOTINI: You're capable of anything.

ELECTRA: I'll be on my bike and out of here like a shot.

ALEKA: Oh, my God!

ELECTRA: Like zooom, in and out of traffic.

FOTINI: Girl, just don't get you started!

ELECTRA: Didn't you say they've put him with the riffraff?

ALEKA: (*despairing*) Oh my God!

FOTINI: (*to E*) Just don't get you started!

ELECTRA: All hell's gonna break loose. (*She starts pedalling again.*)

ALEKA: Something's going to happen to me today ... I just can't make it ... Something's going to happen.

ELECTRA: Just try walking out that door.

ALEKA: Something's going to happen...

FOTINI: She's beside herself. She'll stop at nothing.

ALEKA: I'm not going to make it ...

ELECTRA: All hell's gonna break loose.

FOTINI: I believe her.

ELECTRA: (*getting up*) I'm going to tear everything apart. Tubes, casts, the works.

FOTINI: The works!

ALEKA: Have you both gone crazy?

ELECTRA: To get rid of him at last!

ALEKA: Hold on, Electra ... Listen to me. Let me explain...

ELECTRA: Where's my helmet?

ALEKA: Don't do that, dear...

ELECTRA: That's the last straw.

ALEKA: No, now ... just a minute ... Please...

ELECTRA: The last straw!

ALEKA: Let me explain...

ELECTRA: And I'll stuff him with artichokes.

ALEKA: I just can't make it ... Something is going to happen to me. I cannot make it through this!

FOTINI: Why are you carrying on like this? Didn't he just drop you and leave? He's a bastard and should pay!

ALEKA: That's not exactly the way things are...

FOTINI: Didn't he humiliate you? Didn't he trash you for no reason?

ALEKA: Fotini, dear, Stefano isn't to blame...

ELECTRA: Where's my helmet?

FOTINI: Over behind the armchair.

ALEKA: Stefano is innocent.

FOTINI: Show no mercy ... Show no mercy whatsoever!

ALEKA: Stefano is not to blame ... I ... I am to blame for everything.

FOTINI: So subservient? So very subservient?

ALEKA: I'm to blame. Because what the Maestro said ... had some truth in it.

FOTINI: Of course there's truth in it. You have a most beautiful ass. We know that. It shows.

ALEKA: Yes, but that wasn't all he told him. He told him something else...

FOTINI: What else? What else?

ALEKA: He didn't live up to the faith I put in him ... Because when I agreed to have a cup of coffee with him ... I trusted him ....

FOTINI: What?

ALEKA: I showed faith in him, do you understand?

FOTINI: No I don't understand...

ELECTRA: No need to. Let it go. (*She throws the helmet on the couch.*)

FOTINI: Hold on ... You had coffee? What coffee?

ELECTRA: What coffee, Fotini? ... Espresso...

FOTINI: Ahaaa...

ALEKA: So don't blame Stefano...

FOTINI: You mean, he fucked you?

ALEKA: Aaah!

FOTINI: What I mean to say is ... Ahaaa!

(*Pause.* ALEKA *cries.*)

ELECTRA: It looks like I'm gonna to fucking start feeling sorry for Stefano any minute now.

ALEKA: Do you understand now, Electra? Do you understand that Stefano isn't about to come back?

ELECTRA: Oh, Mom ... How could you screw up like that?

ALEKA: He's not about to come back...

ELECTRA: You really fucked up.

FOTINI: Ohhh! What a headache I have! What a headache!

6

The next evening. MARO, ALEKA *and* FOTINI *are drinking ouzo.*

MARO: So tell me, how could you make such a stupid mistake?

ALEKA: It was a crucial moment. Who was going to get the role of Alfredo ... It had become a big issue at the Opera ... Stefanos or Kokinakis? Stefanos or Kokinakis? And we were really going through hell, and I kept asking myself, what can I do, God, to help him have that chance ... Because only a chance like that can get you to the top. Do you understand? That's what was torturing me ... And as I was waiting for Stefanos in the foyer ... call it luck, call it my thought projections ... the Maestro approached me ... He approached me, I didn't approach him ... And he started talking to me about Stefano's talent ... and about how unfairly he's been treated ... And I was thinking about that role. That's all I could think of. And I was thinking, 'How can I tell him? How can I broach the subject?' Because he's the one who runs things.

MARO: Patriarcheas?

ALEKA: He's got the power.

MARO: Ohhh.

ALEKA: And suddenly he grabs me by the arm and says

'Coffee. Quick, let's get a cup of coffee.'

FOTINI: The son of a bitch!

ALEKA: I was stunned ... I wasn't expecting that, see? But I thought, 'This is Stefano's big chance. The chance of a lifetime!' ...

And I take a deep breath and I say, 'Let's have coffee but we'll drink to Stefano's career.'

MARO: And you went?

(*Pause*)

ALEKA: He had this huge villa, at Anavisso ... and on the walls there were portraits of Callas, and Tito Gobbi ... Pavarotti, and so on ... And I said to him, 'That's the kind of career I dream about for Stefanos'. And in answer he opens a bottle of champagne...

FOTINI: Then what?

ALEKA: Then he sat at the piano and started playing ... the preludes...

MARO: The preludes?

ALEKA: Preludes ... Preludes and preludes ... In the meantime I kept on drinking champagne ... Until opposite us, through that glass window ... that big glass window, the sun started setting ... and that sun was sinking into the sea. And you know how I am about sunsets.

MARO: I know, I know...

ALEKA: ... and the sun sinking into the sea...

MARO: I know.

ALEKA: And that was it.

MARO: Do you remember Skopelos with that Italian...

ALEKA: Anyway ... so much for that ... (*She lights a cigarette.*)

(*Pause*)

MARO: So that's how he got the role of Alfredo...

ALEKA: That's how.

MARO: I see...

ALEKA: And stop reminding me of that Italian. No matter what I say to you, you say, 'with that Italian'.

MARO: I apologize.

(Pause)

FOTINI: And after that?

ALEKA: After that it got to be a habit.

FOTINI: How long did it last?

ALEKA: Two months...

MARO: Two months?

FOTINI: He was insatiable!

MARO: To tell you the truth, he does have a certain charm...

ALEKA: Aaah!... And the closer it got to opening night the more excited he became! 'You're driving me crazy with the games you play ... I'm going to hang myself with the tie you gave me...'

MARO: Aaa!

ALEKA: 'I'll commit suicide hugging your purple panties.'

MARO: Aaa!

ALEKA: And more, lots more ... Until he went totally berserk and told Stefano everything.

FOTINI: The son of a bitch!

ALEKA: Everything!

MARO: And Stefano must have...

ALEKA: Stefano ... 'You made a fool out of me,' he said ... 'You turned me into a laughing stock' ... and he got up and walked out ... Those were his last words ... He put on his trench coat and left ... *(She cries.)*

(FOTINI takes a tissue from a packet on the table and hands it to her.)

FOTINI: Go ahead and cry ... Get it out of your system.

MARO: So what's happening now?

FOTINI: What's happening? Nothing's happening.

ALEKA: He doesn't even turn to look at me. Not even to look at me.

FOTINI: Like she doesn't exist, understand?

ALEKA: All last night and all day today I waited for one word ... one look.

MARO: Nothing?

ALEKA: Nothing.

FOTINI: He doesn't even want to look at her.

ALEKA: I'm sorry, girls ... It's got me down. I can't get hold of myself.

FOTINI: Cry ... Get it out of your system.

(*Pause*)

MARO: What a terrible thing to happen!

FOTINI: Yeah, but she played games with him...

MARO: What games?

FOTINI: Didn't you hear? She played games with him.

MARO: Ah! She played games...

ALEKA: What games? What are you talking about?

FOTINI: 'You're driving me crazy with the games you play.' Isn't that what he told you?

ALEKA: He was in love...

FOTINI: And you played games with him.

MARO: What did you do to him?

ALEKA: Me?

FOTINI: (*laughs*) Come on, tell us now ... what did you do to him?

ALEKA: Nothing ... I talked to him a lot about Stefano.

MARO: About Stefano?

FOTINI: I don't believe it!

ALEKA: Not once did I deny my devotion to Stefano.

MARO: Even while you were making love?

ALEKA: Constantly ... Constantly...

FOTINI: Well, that's why he went crazy.

ALEKA: He was competitive ... Very competitive...

MARO: But on the other hand you, Aleka, went much too far ... Two months?

FOTINI: You spent two months talking to him about Stefano?

ALEKA: What can I do? What can I do? (*She cries.*)

MARO: So now what do we do?

FOTINI: Now we drink ouzo.

MARO: We have to do something.

FOTINI: There's nothing we can do. Believe me.

MARO: That's not possible. There must be something we can do.

FOTINI: Given the character that Stefano has?

MARO: Let's think it over ... Let's talk it through.

FOTINI: There's nothing to be done, Maro. Now she has to protect her dignity. Enough's enough. She cried, tore her cheeks, beat her breast ... It's enough!

ALEKA: How am I going to bear this? How will I bear it?

FOTINI: We'll get on a plane and go. That's what we'll do ... Enough's enough. There's such a thing as dignity.

MARO: Hold it right there, Fotini ... Things aren't all that simple. She is telling you he didn't turn to look at her. Isn't that what you said?

ALEKA: As if I didn't exist...

MARO: Fine, now is that natural? Is it? It isn't.

FOTINI: What do you mean it isn't? After what she did to him?

MARO: Not even a glance? Nothing? What meaning does nothing have? Nothing has a meaning. Nothing has a meaning.

FOTINI: What meaning does it have, exactly?

MARO: He's afraid one look will put him under her spell again.

ALEKA: Do you think so?

MARO: Don't doubt it for a minute. That's what it is.

ALEKA: That's why he avoids looking at me...

MARO: That's exactly why. But how long can he hold out? That moment will come when he'll let his guard down and look you in the eyes. Once he's looked? He's finished.

ALEKA: Oh, Maro...

MARO: But you have to bombard him with your presence. Did you take him flowers?

ALEKA: I've filled the room with flowers.

MARO: Good. You're going to take him some more.

FOTINI: Yeah, but if the other one told him about the purple panties...

MARO: That's beside the point, Fotini. Artists love flowers.

ALEKA: They love them, they love them, they really do.

MARO: That's what I'm telling you. And you're going to bombard him with your presence. Constantly.

ALEKA: I won't leave his side.

MARO: Not for an instant. Until he gives in.

ALEKA: I'm with you.

MARO: The nurses will ask you to leave, the doctors will get angry with you ... But you don't budge. You stay, stay, stay, stay. Until he gives in...

ALEKA: I understand.

MARO: ...and falls into your arms.

ALEKA: Oh Maro!

FOTINI: What does this mean? We start a new theme song now? Will he give in – won't he give in? Will he gives in? – won't he give in?

MARO: Oh come on, Fotini, why are you acting like that? In five days he will have given in.

FOTINI: Five days?

MARO: At the most.

FOTINI: Oh no you don't! Five days is too much.

ALEKA: It's not too much, Fotini, dear...

FOTINI: I can't take any more of this. I can't. I'm starting to feel extremely agitated!

MARO: Well, you're going to be patient five more days.

FOTINI: Yeah, sure ... and five days will go by ... and then you'll both start in: he didn't look at her on Saturday – he'll look at her on Monday ... I know the two of you all too well. I'm onto your tricks. And here I'll be locked in playing solitaire! Will he call her Alekoushka? – won't he call her Alekoushka? Will he call her Alekoushka? – won't he call her Alekoushka?

(ELECTRA *enters. She is holding a large transparent bag from an expensive sweets shop filled with assorted chocolates.*)

ALEKA: (*she sees* E) What's that?

ELECTRA: I found it in the garden.

MARO: Chocolates!

ELECTRA: I found it in the garden. It was hanging on the orange tree.

FOTINI: Aaa! Anthony!

MARO: (*joyfully*) Anthony!

FOTINI: Anthony has discovered me!

(ELECTRA *leaves the bag on the coffee table in front of them.*)

MARO: Would you look at this! Oh, my goodness!

FOTINI: Oh, the bastard! The son of a bitch! He discovered me!

ALEKA: Pretty colours!

FOTINI: So now what do we do?

ELECTRA: We're going to eat them all up.

FOTINI: Are you crazy? You go put them back right now! Right where you found them.

ELECTRA: Come on, what's with you?

FOTINI: Electra, put them back where you found them ... You know nothing, you've seen nothing. Put them back where you found them.

ALEKA: What chocolates are they?

MARO: Assorted...

ALEKA: Let me see ... Because when I cry, I do like something sweet afterwards ... (*She starts to untie the ribbon.*)

FOTINI: Don't touch those!

ELECTRA: Oh, come on ... Give us a break...

FOTINI: You go put those back where you found them right now.

ELECTRA: If I put them back, he's going to know that you're here and that you told me to put them back ... But if we keep them – we kept them. You don't know anything.

FOTINI: Don't give me a hard time, just don't upset me!

ELECTRA: Look, I'm the one who found them. Did you go out at all into the garden?

FOTINI: I did not go out...

ELECTRA: So I took them – I ate them. (*She grabs the bag and unties the ribbon.*)

MARO: That's right.

ALEKA: But when did he put them in the garden?

FOTINI: Didn't I tell you he'd find me?

MARO: He must have seen your car.

FOTINI: What car? I came here in a taxi. From Lycabettus. Don't you remember?

MARO: Oh, right...

ALEKA: And he hung them on the orange tree ... (*She laughs.*) Oh really Fotini, and you say he wants to kill you ...

ELECTRA: Let's see, then, what chocolates do we have here? (*She empties the bag on the table.*)

(*They all examine the chocolates, with the exception of* FOTINI.)

ELECTRA: Let's see ... What's this one called? 'Flame' ...

FOTINI: Flame? No, no, no. Take that away!

ELECTRA: Why?

FOTINI: Take it away! Take it away!

ELECTRA: It has liqueur in the centre.

FOTINI: Look, now, I know what I'm saying. It looks like liqueur ... but it isn't.

ELECTRA: It isn't? (*She reads.*) It says here Cointreau.

FOTINI: I mean, it is liqueur ... but it isn't just liqueur. It's liqueur and something else ...

ELECTRA: Oooh! Let me see. (*She unwraps the chocolate.*)

FOTINI: Electra, don't!

ELECTRA: (*bites into it*) Mmmm ...

FOTINI: Electra, be careful. They're an aphrodisiac.

MARO: Aphrodisiac?

ALEKA: Which, this one? (*She takes one of the same.*)

FOTINI: Yes, that one.

MARO: Let me see ... is it Flame?

FOTINI: Do you see what he does? He sends me those on purpose, the son of a bitch.

ELECTRA: Mmm ... It's good! When I go see Jason I'll be turned on and ready to go.

FOTINI: There's another one ... An orange one ... Let's see ... (*She looks for it.*) A Spanish one ... Here it is!

MARO: This one?

FOTINI: This one. This one's even worse!

ALEKA: Well then let's try it. (*She takes the chocolate, breaks it in two, and gives half to* MARO.)

ELECTRA: Let's give some to Stefano. It may make him turn and look at her ...

MARO: Let me have some.

ALEKA: Nice taste ... strange...

MARO: Strange ... Nice.

FOTINI: Just wait and you'll see.

(*Pause. They eat.*)

FOTINI: How do you feel?

ALEKA: Funny...

FOTINI: Didn't I tell you? (*She takes a piece also.*)

MARO: That's nice! ... Real nice! Now if we just had Alain Delon in his prime!

(*They laugh.*)

7

Six days later. It's three in the morning. The stage is dark. The doorbell rings. ALEKA *comes down in her nightgown.*

ALEKA: Who is it?

MARO: It's me, Aleka, Maro.

(ALEKA *opens the door.* MARO *enters.*)

MARO: (*happy*) He came, Aleka! He came!

ALEKA: He came?

MARO: He came!

ALEKA: The blond?

MARO: He came, Aleka! He came! (*She falls into* ALEKA's *arms.*)

ALEKA: I can't believe it ... When did he come?

MARO: This afternoon.

ALEKA: This afternoon.

MARO: I was on my way out. I was going to the travel agency to pick up the tickets...

ALEKA: Aaaa ... Did you get them?

MARO: No I didn't make it.

ALEKA: Well, thank goodness for that!

MARO: I was putting on my earrings, and as I turned to leave, I saw him standing there in front of me...

ALEKA: Just like that.

MARO: Just like that!

ALEKA: That's it!

MARO: I was putting on my earrings . . . and I let out a cry
– aaaa!

ALEKA: Those things happen suddenly.

MARO: Just think, one minute later . . . and it wouldn't have
happened!

ALEKA: Oh, my God!

MARO: Do you see? In other words, if I weren't still there
putting on my earrings . . .

ALEKA: It wouldn't have happened . . .

MARO: In other words it was a matter of seconds.

ALEKA: So what happened?

MARO: Everything! Everything!

ALEKA: You mean like you had imagined?

MARO: Much more!

ALEKA: Well come on, tell me . . .

   (*They sit.*)

MARO: Much more!

ALEKA: I have news too . . .

MARO: About Stefano?

ALEKA: I have to tell you.

MARO: What?

   (FOTINI *appears. She descends the stairs.*)

ALEKA: I'll tell you later . . .

   (*An awkward pause*)

FOTINI: What's going on?

MARO: He came . . .

FOTINI: He came? Who came?

ALEKA: The blond! He came!

FOTINI: He came?

MARO: Remember us saying it, Fotini? 'Will he come? –
won't he come? Will he come? – won't he come?'

ALEKA: So what happened? What happened?

MARO: What happened?

FOTINI: He came. Then what happened?

MARO: I don't remember. I don't remember a thing...

ALEKA: You don't remember?

MARO: If you're asking me to tell you what happened from the instant I saw him in front of me and he says, 'Let's go for a ride' ... how it happened, what happened ... how long it took to close the shop ... how I ended up in a jeep speeding along the freeway, destination unknown ... I really couldn't say...

ALEKA: The freeway?

MARO: I don't know how I got there...

ALEKA: You were in shock...

MARO: I was in shock ... It was no small matter...

ALEKA: Are you kidding? So suddenly like that...

MARO: And how I ended up suddenly on Eliki – I haven't the slightest idea.

FOTINI: On Eliki? Which Eliki?

MARO: The lake.

ALEKA: The lake?

FOTINI: Where our drinking water comes from?

MARO: Where our drinking water comes from.

ALEKA: Well isn't that illegal?

MARO: Aleka, my darling, he's mad! He's wonderful!

ALEKA: And what did you do on Lake Eliki?

MARO: Well, there we were racing along the freeway, when suddenly he stops the jeep and says 'Get out' ... I ask him, 'What are we going to do here?' He says, 'Wait,' and he takes a big box from the car like that ... a long black suitcase ... he takes it with him ... he takes me by the hand ... and says, 'Let's go'...

ALEKA: And then?

MARO: We walk down the embankment ... we jump over some barbed wire and we get down to the lake ... That's when he opens the box ... he presses a button ... and, whoosh, out pops a boat!

ALEKA: Aaaa!

MARO: A yellow inflatable boat ... and he says, 'Come on'...

ALEKA: And you weren't afraid?

MARO: I was afraid, but I couldn't say no to him.

FOTINI: That's the trouble with you. You can't say no. You just can't say no. (*She lights a cigarette.*)

MARO: ...

ALEKA: So then what?

MARO: Anyway, the Eliki we see passing by on the freeway is nothing like what you see when you're on it ... Once you're there it's a different Eliki...

ALEKA: Really?

MARO: Inside it has levels ...

FOTINI: Levels? What levels?

MARO: At the bottom ... it has horizontal levels you can lie down on...

ALEKA: No kidding!

MARO: That's right ... They're like lounge chairs on the bottom.

ALEKA: Imagine that!

MARO: And such stillness I mean, you have never seen such stillness in your life.

ALEKA: There, that's the sort of thing I'm crazy about!

MARO: I mean, it's a terrific experience – Lake Eliki.

ALEKA: I just love things like that...

MARO: In the meantime he didn't even talk.

FOTINI: He didn't talk?

MARO: After we had made love and the moon came up he started to talk...

ALEKA: It seems he's the quiet type...

MARO: He's a man of few words...

FOTINI: That's all well and good, but how does he know those places?

MARO: How should I know?

FOTINI: Because it looks like he knew where he was going.

MARO: It looks like he knew...

FOTINI: I mean he's been there before.

MARO: He's been there before. What can I say? That's what it looked like to me.

FOTINI: In other words he's turned Lake Eliki into a bachelor pad?

MARO: How should I know?

ALEKA: I'll go mad! (*She laughs.*)

MARO: At any rate, girls, he so at ease. He has such style ...
Like, say, when he drives ... he held the steering wheel
with one hand and me with the other, while he kissed me.

ALEKA: Like Elvis Presley.

MARO: Nothing like Elvis Presley ... He was a chubby little
baby, I'm talking about a man with incredible angles in his
face!

ALEKA: Aaaa!

MARO: And his eyes are a combination of velvet and steel!

ALEKA: Steel has a blue tint...

MARO: That's it. Steel blue.

ALEKA: I'm getting the picture...

MARO: For an instant I even said to myself ... I said, 'If I
am meant to die from the beauty of those eyes ... then let
me die!'

FOTINI: Maybe he gave you a little something?

MARO: Nothing.

FOTINI: Not even some hash ... nothing?

MARO: Nothing.

ALEKA: What are you saying, girl! You really found yourself
that kind of man!

MARO: It's what I've always wanted, Aleka.

ALEKA: If you're talking to me about steel-blue...

MARO: What I've always wanted!

ALEKA: So tell me. Is he a pilot after all?

MARO: He's not a pilot.

ALEKA: Oh, he's not a pilot...

FOTINI: So what does he do?

MARO: He's the grandson of an industrialist.

ALEKA: Oh, my! I'm really curious to meet him.

MARO: I'll bring him over. I'll bring him to meet you.

ALEKA: Look how red her cheeks are! Look at her skin ...
She's glowing!

MARO: Really, is that true?

ALEKA: It's because she's in love.

MARO: Let me see ... (*She goes and looks in the mirror.*)

ALEKA: You're beautiful!

MARO: I'm happy, girls! I'm really happy!

FOTINI: Tell me something Maro . . . Did you get the tickets?

MARO: The tickets?

FOTINI: The tickets, for the trip, did you get them?

MARO: I didn't have time.

FOTINI: What do you mean you didn't have time?

MARO: The moment I was putting on my earrings to go, Hector came.

FOTINI: OK, so when do you think you'll be getting them?

MARO: Fotini dear . . .

ALEKA: Shouldn't you be saying its a good thing she didn't get them?

FOTINI: I don't understand . . .

ALEKA: Because with things like that . . . you know how it is . . . Once you buy the tickets – just try getting your money back.

MARO: Don't even mention it.

ALEKA: Are you kidding?

MARO: No way! Don't even mention it.

FOTINI: Yes, but didn't we say yesterday to get the tickets so we could leave?

MARO: Now that Hector's come, you want me to leave? To go where?

ALEKA: Are you kidding?

MARO: I'm not about to leave.

ALEKA: And what about me? Do you think I can leave?

MARO: It's totally out of the question.

ALEKA: What about me? Do you want me to tell you? Well, today I saw a tear!

MARO: A tear? What tear?

ALEKA: A tear rolled down his cheek.

MARO: That's it! He's starting to give in!

ALEKA: One tear and he looked at me . . .

MARO: He looked at you?

ALEKA: For about five or six seconds . . .

MARO: I see.

ALEKA: As long as it takes for one tear to fall.

MARO: Well now, how can you possibly leave?

ALEKA: How can I leave?

MARO: Can you leave at a time like this? Now he's just beginning to give in.

ALEKA: And I asked the head-nurse. I said to her, 'Does that tear come from physical or emotional pain?' 'What can I tell you,' she answered. 'In here those two get confused...'

MARO: Yeah, well, that we already know.

ALEKA: That's what she said.

MARO: Don't give it a second thought. He's beginning to break.

ALEKA: Do you really think so?

MARO: It's certain.

ALEKA: I'll go mad, Maro! (*She falls into her arms.*)

MARO: Aleka, my darling!

ALEKA: I'll go mad!

MARO: Didn't I tell you he'd come round?

ALEKA: You said he would.

MARO: Didn't I tell you?

ALEKA: Yes, you did, Maro, you did.

FOTINI: So now what happens to me? (*Pause*) What happens to me? I've been shut up in here a week now ... and it's driving me crazy ... I'm not the type of person who stays indoors ... Do you know that? Are you aware of that? (*Pause*) I want to go outside! To breathe fresh air. I can't stand being closed up in here, in this prison!

ALEKA: What prison?

FOTINI: The two of you go running around from one place to the next and here I sit, imprisoned, brushing my teeth with last year's toothbrush. And I wait ... Will the blond come? – won't the blond come? Then there's the other one, will he call her Alekoushka? – won't he call her Alekoushka? When will he call her Alekoushka? I can't take any more postponements. I can't take any more postponements!

MARO: Well then, what would you have us do?

FOTINI: I just can't!

ALEKA: Fotini, dear, we had no intention of...

FOTINI: These postponements are killing me. Lake Eliki has
    levels, she says ... It has lounge chairs...

MARO: (*getting riled*) Now you listen here...

ALEKA: (*winking conspiratorially at* MARO) Things just turn
    out that way sometimes...

FOTINI: (*to* A) Why did you wink at her? Would you please
    tell me why you winked at her?

ALEKA: Who winked?

FOTINI: You winked at her – just now, I saw you.

ALEKA: Who, me?

FOTINI: You winked at her.

ALEKA: When?

FOTINI: Now, just now. You winked at her.

ALEKA: I winked?

FOTINI: You winked at her, Aleka. I saw you wink at her.

ALEKA: Maro, did I wink at you?

MARO: I didn't see ... I didn't...

FOTINI: Oh, I can't take any more of this! I can't stand it!
    (*She breaks into tears. Pause*) How could I have let this
    happen to me? How could I have let myself depend on the
    two of you? And now what do I do? What do I do now? I
    have to get away from here now ... And how do I do that?

ALEKA: And just why must you leave?

FOTINI: What else can I do? Stay here? I was staying here
    in order to leave. I wasn't staying just to stay here.

ALEKA: What I mean is, no one is asking you to leave. Is
    anyone asking you to leave?

FOTINI: We said we'd take a trip. Didn't we say we'd take
    a trip? What will I do now? What will I do? Go on, you
    tell me now what will I do? (*She cries.*)

MARO: Really, now, how did I get mixed up with this trip? I
    don't even like to travel.

FOTINI: I must find a solution ... I must find a solution...

ALEKA: We'll find the solution. Calm down. (*She caresses
    her.*)

FOTINI: How can I calm down? If I dare set foot out of
    here, I'll walk into his trap. He puts a knife to my throat:
    either you marry me or ... Because I infuriated him. I

infuriated him beyond limits...

ALEKA: Oh, for chrissake ... He's filled the garden full of chocolates. He drives by and tosses bags of chocolate. As if he would put a knife to your throat...

FOTINI: Why, things like that don't happen, Aleka? They don't happen? And suddenly I find myself married. Don't you see? (*She cries.*)

ALEKA: Don't you let anything frighten you. You go meet him head on. When he sees you coming head on, he'll back off.

FOTINI: Who will back off? Anthony?

ALEKA: I'm telling you he will...

FOTINI: You don't know Anthony. He'll put on the pressure. He'll move in on me from all sides. He'll get to me one way or another ... and before you know it, I'll wind up at Vivari again for the weekend. How can I stand it? He'll get me back into the same old rut with his spearfishing ... 'I hit two blackfish, I hit three red mullet. Look at that octopus! ... I'll grill it for you over charcoal' ... and we're right back where we started. Then suddenly he gets manic and says, 'I'm not coming out until I hit a gilthead' ... But are those easy to find?

ALEKA: No. The gilthead's a hard fish to catch.

FOTINI: And there I am, sitting on the veranda for hours, looking at magazines. And more magazines ... and more magazines ... And then all of a sudden I get this funny feeling and I start to worry ... I start to worry that a shark will get him. 'Now he's gonna get him ... now he's got him' ... And then I start going crazy because I think that maybe my thoughts will lead the shark to him. Because things like that happen, you know.

ALEKA: Of course they do.

FOTINI: So I try to get my mind off the shark ... I try and I try ... but instead I see the shark approaching him and I go cold with fear...

MARO: Say, are there really sharks at Vivari?

FOTINI: How should I know? Meanwhile I've read that dreadful book you gave me ... The one that says, 'That which we fear is that which we unconsciously desire' and then I really go crazy ... and I start screaming, 'Anthony! Anthony!' No answer... 'Get out of the water ... Get out...'

MARO: Well, how can he hear when he's underwater?

FOTINI: I mean, it's awful ... How can I kill the only person who cares about me?

ALEKA: That's so true ... Because if something did happen to him, you would feel guilty for the rest of your life...

FOTINI: Do you see what he does to me?

ALEKA: I see...

FOTINI: I mean, it's driving me crazy! He's driving me crazy!

8

Several days later. The house is somewhat messy. ELECTRA *is putting her records and cassettes in order.* ALEKA *brings two cups of coffee.*

MARO: I just had this feeling ... 'So perfect! So wonderful! It's not possible! Something's wrong somewhere. It can't be true. Something's wrong somewhere. Something's wrong somewhere, something's wrong somewhere' ... And there it is!

ALEKA: Aren't you glad it came to light before it's too late?

MARO: Did you put sugar in this coffee?

ALEKA: No I didn't put in any sugar.

MARO: It tastes like you did...

ALEKA: Did he come right out and say it?

MARO: No ... not in so many words...

ALEKA: How then?

MARO: Look what happened. We went for a drive today ... to the Flea Market at Monastiraki. Now, I don't know, I could be overreacting...

ALEKA: Go on, tell me.

MARO: And as we were walking around down there just

browsing ... It was in one of those helmets – turned upside down – they were just some old army medals for sale. In this store. When suddenly he stops and begins looking through those medals. He chooses one and asks, 'How much is this?' The guy says, 'One thousand drachma' ... And yours truly pulls out three thousand and hands them to him.

ALEKA: Three thousand?

MARO: The guy in the store was stunned. He goes 'But' ... and Hector says, 'It's not even enough. Really, it's nothing. Because this medal,' he says, 'was the biggest honor that could be bestowed by the Third Reich. The Führer awarded it personally, and to very few.'

ALEKA: Oh, really?

MARO: And there was a man nearby who heard all this. A short little guy, that tall ... and he goes over to this other guy and says to him, 'Things are getting bad. The country's overrun with Nazis.'

ALEKA: He said that?

MARO: It's overrun with Nazis.

ALEKA: And what was the medal like?

MARO: A regular medal. Yours truly takes it, put it in his pocket and says to me, 'Let's go.'

ALEKA: Maybe he's a collector...

MARO: Oh God, I hope so!

ALEKA: He's probably a collector.

MARO: Now wait until you hear the rest of it. Before we got to the Flea Market, we had walked past the ancient Agora. 'Let's go,' he says, 'and see the Titans.'

ALEKA: Which Titans?

MARO: They're these statues, Aleka, in the ancient Agora.

ALEKA: Aaaaa...

MARO: And he stood there marveling at the Titans ... And he kept saying, 'Those giants! Those giants!' ... I didn't pay much attention to it at the time. Now I do though. Now I do. And he kept talking about the 'size', the 'size' 'the size and the power' ... 'those gigantic proportions overwhelm me' ...

ALEKA: He said that?

MARO: 'These mutilated giants just break my heart'...

ALEKA: Oh my, do you think he's a Nazi?

MARO: That's what I'm afraid of, Aleka, he just may be!

ALEKA: Because that bit about the giants ... The medal ... somehow ... At least you can say ... he's a collector – maybe.

MARO: But the giants? Breaking his heart?

ALEKA: Oh, my! What have you got yourself into!

ELECTRA: Tell me something, Maro ... Did you mention anything afterwards?

MARO: Mention what?

ELECTRA: Anything about the medal and...

MARO: No, I didn't.

ELECTRA: Did you hint at anything?

MARO: No, nothing...

ELECTRA: That's good. You just saved your own life. Thank goodness for that ... But now you have to disappear.

MARO: Disappear?

ELECTRA: Because if he tells you his secret – you're done for. Thank God he didn't tell you. But you're in danger of him telling you. That I'm such and such ... and I belong to this organization – let's say ... If that happens, you're done for. You're inducted into the system and you get a code number: 242ZKR. And then you receive assignments.

ALEKA: My word girl, what are you mixed up in!

ELECTRA: And then you can't back out, you can't say I'm leaving ... As soon as you say the words – you're dead!

ALEKA: Oh my God!

MARO: So what do I do now?

ALEKA: Disappear, Maro. Disappear.

MARO: How do I disappear?

ELECTRA: Instantaneously.

MARO: But we have a date ... to go to Sounio. He's coming at five o'clock to pick me up...

ELECTRA: You won't be there.

MARO: But where would I go? I have my studio ... I have my work.

ELECTRA: How important is that now? Your life is in danger.

MARO: Oh, my God! What have I got myself into?

ALEKA: You have to disappear, Maro. Disappear from sight.

MARO: Where can I go?

ALEKA: You can stay here.

MARO: Here? You want me to stay closed up in here? Didn't you see what happened to Fotini?

ALEKA: What happened to Fotini?

MARO: And besides, you play loud music ... and I can't stand it ... And Stefano singing those arias. I've heard them two hundred times ... I can't take that any more.

ELECTRA: So go to Thailand.

ALEKA: Will you stop going on about Thailand? We're not going to Thailand. That's final. But I know what you're up to. You're hoping I'll leave so you can bring that film crew in here. Well, you can just make up your mind to it. I'm not leaving. I'm not going anywhere.

(*Pause*)

MARO: It's my bad luck. I know it. I will never find someone who's right for me ... I will never find a man who's right for me ... (*She cries.*)

ALEKA: Oh, come now ... You can't stop hoping...

MARO: Maybe I'm to blame, do you think? I'm starting to believe it's all my fault. I attract these deviants. That's what happens you know. You know that's probably what it is.

ALEKA: Oh, come now. Really...

MARO: What else can I believe? Do you remember that big time lawyer? 'This way, please' and 'That way, please' ... and 'That way, please' ... and 'This way, please' ... and 'That way, please'...

ALEKA: I had told you at the time, 'Beware the man who wears a suit with wide stripes'.

ELECTRA: (*hamming it up*) 'This way please,' and 'That way please' and 'That way please.'

MARO: What about that other one who had the craving for pig-knuckle soup? We'd comb the whole of Attica looking for what he called, 'the best pig-knuckle soup' ... 'the best pig-knuckle soup!' ...

ELECTRA: Ha ha ...

MARO: We went as far as Thebes once.

ALEKA: You're talking about that strange one.

ELECTRA: Say, when was all this going on? It's the first I've heard of it.

ALEKA: The one with the little Alfa Romeo.

MARO: I had dumped Fatso again ... and Electra, my dear, I ran smack into that one. 'The best pig-knuckle soup' ... 'The best pig-knuckle soup.'

ELECTRA: No shit!

MARO: Then one day, what do you think he says to me? 'The mother of all pig-knuckle soups is of course Salonica' ... My blood ran cold ... 'But the best of all pig-knuckle soups is made by Suleiman in Komotini.'

(*They laugh.*)

ELECTRA: Really I don't believe it!

MARO: Well, I tell him he can go alone to eat that soup. And good riddance. It was a narrow escape ...

ELECTRA: That's an incredible story.

MARO: His name was Pericles ... and now there's this one ...

ALEKA: Maybe you're just too easygoing.

MARO: ...

ALEKA: You're a pushover, Maro. They can see it in your eyes.

(*Pause*)

MARO: Why does this have to happen to me, God, why ... Just when I found someone I really want, why does this have to happen ... (*She jumps up.*) Do you think we should have him over?

ALEKA: Have who over?

MARO: Hector.

ALEKA: What are you talking about?

MARO: So you can meet him too ...

ALEKA: You want me to invite a Nazi into my home?

MARO: We may be making a mistake, Aleka dear...

ALEKA: It's out of the question.

MARO: We may be getting way off track. Just because some little man happened along. Let's look into it ... Let's examine the situation.

ALEKA: Oh, no you don't! Things like that frighten me.

MARO: Let's not condemn the man...

ALEKA: I said no!

MARO: Aleka, I feel the same way you do about this ... I can't stand Nazis. But if you trust my intuition.

ALEKA: I'm telling you, it's not possible...

MARO: Why not, the more I think of it, he can't – he's wonderful, you know? Polite ... tender ... tactful ... a gentleman! He doesn't ask questions, he doesn't make demands or anything.

ALEKA: It's absolutely out of the question. That sort of thing frightens me.

MARO: Yes, but let's just look into it ... Let's find out more about him...

ALEKA: Not on your life, Maro. You just make sure you disappear.

MARO: Yes, but if he's a Nazi and I disappear, I've had it. He'll say I dumped him, and then I'm in real trouble.

ALEKA: I hadn't thought of that...

MARO: Do you see? He'll say I got the message then dumped him.

ALEKA: And those Nazis are vindictive.

MARO: That's what frightens me, Aleka, don't you see? How long can I disappear?

ALEKA: So what do we do now?

MARO: How should I know? We think.

ALEKA: And what conclusions do you reach?

MARO: I shouldn't aggravate him.

ALEKA: Which means?

MARO: Perhaps I should take it easy...

ALEKA: Take it easy?

MARO: So I won't aggravate him, understand?

ALEKA: I understand. To phase out, as they say.

MARO: Slowly...

ALEKA: 'I m not in the mood for sex ... Let it go today, and tomorrow we'll see'...

MARO: That's it exactly, Aleka...

ALEKA: And 'Let's go out to dinner instead'...

MARO: ...It's hard ... Really hard...

ALEKA: Anyway. You're going to try.

MARO: I'm going to try ... I'll fight this.

ALEKA: You'll give in – then pull away. You'll give in – then pull away. Until finally he'll short-circuit completely and send you to hell. That's the only solution. Good thinking, Maro!

ELECTRA: In the meantime I'll throw Vivian his way for diversion.

MARO: Who's Vivian?

ELECTRA: This incredible female, blonde, blue eyed ... Perfect ... Just his type...

ALEKA: Who is she? Do I know her?

ELECTRA: You know Vivian, Mother, from my class at school.

ALEKA: Oh, yes ... Good idea!

ELECTRA: You know, there's not been one male yet able to resist her!

ALEKA: She's perfect. Good!

ELECTRA: And she's not afraid of anything. She dives right in!

MARO: No, Electra, dear. It's not necessary.

ELECTRA: I want to help you.

MARO: It's not necessary ... I'll go this one alone.

ELECTRA: So you'll be safe once and for all.

MARO: I'll give in – I'll pull away. I'll give in – I'll pull away...

ALEKA: Just be sure you're through with this in a week.

MARO: Well, I'm off now so I'll have time to shower, because he's coming in half an hour.

ALEKA: Start phasing out.

MARO: Sure, OK...

ALEKA: Starting from today.

MARO: OK, I will...

ALEKA: And in one week –

MARO: Right, okay...

ALEKA: Because it won't do to drag things out.

MARO: OK. OK...

ALEKA: You know...

MARO: I know, I know ... Well, bye now ... (*She opens the door.*)

ELECTRA: Look if you should happen to need Vivian.

MARO: Will you stop harping on about this Vivian? Vivian, Vivian, Vivian...

ELECTRA: Ha ha ha...

ALEKA: That's enough, now...

MARO: This Vivian does not interest me.

ELECTRA: Ha ha ha...

ALEKA: Go on, leave. Because I have to get ready to go to the hospital...

MARO: Vivian, Vivian, Vivian ... (*She leaves.*)

ELECTRA: (*playfully*) I'll give in – I'll pull away. I'll give in – I'll pull away.

9

A few days later. Afternoon.

FOTINI: I broke down! As soon as I saw him with that speargun I went to pieces!

ALEKA: It was just too much for you.

FOTINI: I went to pieces. I was beside myself. 'I can't stand Vivari any more. It's always Vivari, Vivari' ... And we were out of there in no time at all.

MARO: Really ... how he is about that place...

ALEKA: I know ... He's absolutely crazy about Vivari...

MARO: It's just awful.

FOTINI: What didn't he hear from me! He had an earful by the time we reached Athens.

ALEKA: I can imagine...

FOTINI: Well, wasn't I justified? Wasn't I? And then in order to get on my good side...

ELECTRA: He stuffed you with chocolates.

FOTINI: Chocolates and this ... 'If you don't like Vivari ... then I'll sell the house there'...

MARO: No kidding!

FOTINI: And 'If you don't want us to get married ... we won't get married ... And no more being afraid of me and hiding at Aleka's house'...

ALEKA: In other words, a lamb.

FOTINI: And 'Of course I love Aleka ... And I'm sorry she's suffering ... and something must be done.' And to make a long story short – he went and saw Stefano.

ALEKA: What?

FOTINI: He got up and went to the hospital.

ALEKA: To the hospital?

FOTINI: This morning.

ALEKA: What are you saying?

FOTINI: Of course, to show an interest, see?

ALEKA: And what happened?

FOTINI: Well, he grabs Stefano and he says, 'What's all this crap? Over a pair of purple panties'...

ALEKA: (embarassed) Eeee!

FOTINI: 'Over a pair of purple panties,' he says, 'you're torturing the woman who adores you as if you were a god?'

ALEKA: He said that?

FOTINI: 'And you sit there,' he says, 'and listen to Patriarcheas stories?'

ALEKA: Oh, the sweetheart!

MARO: There, that's what Anthony has in him! Understand? He has this sensitivity.

FOTINI: He did it to get on my good side.

ALEKA: And Stefano? What did Stefano say to him?

FOTINI: Stefano told him. 'If Aleka weren't feeling guilty ... if she were innocent, say ... would she be hanging around here? At the hospital, all day? She wouldn't be hanging around. She'd get fed up and she'd tell me to go to hell!'

ALEKA: Oh, my God!

MARO: Well, for goodness sake!

FOTINI: Exactly. At that point Anthony got really mad and let him have it. 'Now,' he says, 'you are describing the future. Because that is exactly what Aleka is going to do. She's going to leave you and she's going on a trip with her friends.' This was as far as it goes.

ELECTRA: Oh, that was good!

FOTINI: 'She's going to Thailand with her girlfriends, Maro and Fotini.'

ELECTRA: That was really good!

ALEKA: He said that?

MARO: And Stefano?

FOTINI: It shook him up, he said. He was speechless. At first, that is ... because then he said: 'Yeah, sure ... Aleka? She's not going anywhere. She'll be here, hanging around in the halls getting rid of her guilt.'

MARO: Oh, he didn't swallow it.

FOTINI: He didn't swallow it. But Anthony, who always wants to have the last word, said: 'Goodbye, and I'll bring you the photographs of Aleka in Thailand.'

ELECTRA: He's good, that Anthony! He's really good!

FOTINI: For things like that, sure...

ELECTRA: You haven't understood what happened.

MARO: What happened?

ELECTRA: Really, he's a genius! Because, when Stefano sees the photographs, what's he going to do?

ALEKA: What's he going to do?

ELECTRA: He's going to fall into your arms and call you Alekoushka.

ALEKA: Ohh! What are you saying?

ELECTRA: Don't you understand? Don't you get it?

ALEKA: He'll realize his mistake!

ELECTRA: That's what I'm telling you. Anthony is really big time!

MARO: Fine, but where is she going to get the photographs?

ELECTRA: Oh, big deal ... She'll go to Thailand and take the photographs.

MARO: Well, there is that...

ALEKA: I'll go, Maro, I'll go.

ELECTRA: You'll just pop over to Thailand and take a few photographs hugging some Buddha's...

ALEKA: I'll go. What can I do? Since my life's happiness is depending on it, I'll go. I'll take about forty photographs ... there...

ELECTRA: And you stay about fifteen days – because of course, you can't come back right away...

ALEKA: I can't?

ELECTRA: Really, Mother, are you so naïve? If you come back right away, you've ruined everything.

MARO: She's right, Aleka. You can't come back right away.

ELECTRA: And you should leave as soon as possible. Before the effect wears off. Tomorrow morning you get on that plane and go.

ALEKA: Tomorrow morning?

ELECTRA: Before the effect wears off.

MARO: Tomorrow morning, Aleka, dear. Tomorrow morning you get on that plane and go.

ALEKA: Yes, yes. Tomorrow morning! Oh dear! I have to call Maki at the travel agency. (*She goes to the phone.*) Yes, but Anthony said I'm leaving with my friends.

MARO: With your friends?

ALEKA: With Maro and Fotini. Isn't that what Anthony said?

FOTINI: That's what he said.

MARO: I didn't catch that ... I don't understand...

ALEKA: The two of you have to be in the photographs as well.

MARO: I don't get it...

ALEKA: Or else Stefano will think I went with a lover.

MARO: Oh, no...

ALEKA: It's certain.

MARO: So what happens now?

ALEKA: What happens? We have to go to Thailand. There's no other way. We have to take the photographs.

MARO: (*to* F) Tell me something ... Why did Anthony get me mixed up in all this? Why did he get mixed up in it?

FOTINI: What can I say? Think about it ... Talk it over ...

Get your tickets ... because I am definitely not going.

ALEKA: I don't get it.

FOTINI: I'm not up for a trip to Thailand.

ALEKA: But weren't we going to Thailand? Hadn't we planned it?

FOTINI: Now? Like this? With Anthony's approval, and his blessings? I don't want to go.

MARO: Tell me something, Fotini ... Just how did this whole Thailand thing get started?

FOTINI: What do you mean how?

ALEKA: To convince Stefano, Maro...

MARO: And how did he come up with Thailand?

ALEKA: Well, weren't we going to Thailand?

MARO: Yes, but how did Anthony know that?

FOTINI: I told him.

MARO: You told him?

FOTINI: It slipped out while I was going to pieces.

MARO: When was this?

FOTINI: At Vivari.

MARO: You can't control yourself, can you? You simply have no control over yourself.

FOTINI: Yes, but do you know what I suspect? That he did it on purpose.

ALEKA: Who?

FOTINI: Anthony. He did it on purpose in order to send me to Thailand.

ALEKA: No, he did it for Stefano ... So he would believe him...

FOTINI: Stefano my eye. He did it on purpose. Because when I told him, while I was falling apart, that I wanted to go to Thailand with my girlfriends, what do you think he says to me? 'Go' he says, 'It will be good for your nerves.'

MARO: He said that?

FOTINI: Can you imagine?

ALEKA: For him to say so, it would be good for you.

FOTINI: And he comes off looking generous, get it? Supposedly he's giving me a degree of freedom...

MARO: Well, really!

FOTINI: In order to tempt me into marrying him.

MARO: In other words, a hopeless situation.

FOTINI: That's his angle, all right. Now do you see what he does to me?

MARO: It's a hopeless situation! (*She lights a cigarette.*)

ALEKA: Well, what do you expect him to do? He's fighting for you.

FOTINI: He may be fighting for me, but this time he's not getting away with it.

ALEKA: But Fotini, dear, you won't be going for Anthony. Is it Anthony you'll be going for? It's me you'll be going for.

FOTINI: You threw me out.

ALEKA: I threw you out? When?

FOTINI: Without a second thought.

ALEKA: What are you saying?

FOTINI: Without a second thought!

ALEKA: Are you out of your mind?

FOTINI: You kept me here, imprisoned ... 'Now we're leaving, and now we're leaving' ... Ten days locked up in here, I almost went crazy! And then you packed me off to Anthony.

ALEKA: Just listen to that! Listen to what she's saying!

FOTINI: You supposedly saw a tear. Bullshit.

ALEKA: Just listen to her!

FOTINI: And now you have the nerve to ask me to come to Thailand?

MARO: Let me tell you something, Fotini.

FOTINI: I'm not going to Thailand if it kills me!

MARO: Weren't you the one who told Anthony about Thailand? Well, that does it, because now you're going to Thailand.

ALEKA: Maro, leave her alone.

MARO: No, Aleka...

ALEKA: Leave her alone.

MARO: She'll pay for her mistake.

ALEKA: No, Maro, I don't want her to come.

MARO: What do you mean, you don't want her to come?

ALEKA: After what she said to me? That I threw her out?

FOTINI: Without a second thought! Without a second thought!

ALEKA: I don't want you to come, Fotini. I'll go with Maro. We'll leave as soon as possible. Tomorrow morning.

MARO: I can't

ALEKA: What do you mean, you can't? I don't understand...

MARO: Tomorrow we're going to Delphi ... I can't...

ELECTRA: To Delphi? What are you going to do at Delphi?

MARO: He wants us to see the *Charioteer* together ... I can't.

ELECTRA: Okay, then day after tomorrow.

MARO: The day after tomorrow? (*She thinks.*) It's difficult ... It's really difficult...

ALEKA: Now you listen here ... I'm dying this very moment, and you're talking to me about the *Charioteer*?

MARO: I can't go to Thailand, Aleka.

ALEKA: And you're going to sell me out for a Nazi?

FOTINI: Nazi? Who's a Nazi?

MARO: You're the ones who called him a Nazi.

FOTINI: The blond is a Nazi?

MARO: Did I say he was a Nazi?

ALEKA: You're selling me out for a Nazi?

MARO: You and Electra decided he was a Nazi.

ELECTRA: Didn't you tell us he's a Nazi?

MARO: I told you about an incident.

FOTINI: You mean to say he turns out to be a Nazi?

MARO: We don't know that.

ALEKA: Listen, didn't we agree that you get rid of him?

MARO: When I'm sure he's a Nazi, I'll get rid of him.

ALEKA: Just listen to her, would you! And here I am having nightmares every night that you're in danger ... I see you in ditches and ravines ... All night long if you want to know, and I live in agony that you're mixed up with a Nazi and I'm afraid...

FOTINI: Don't be afraid, Aleka ... I met a Nazi last year in Portaria ... The man sat silently in an armchair and was scornful of everything and everyone. Especially of those who smoked. Because they don't have the will power to stop. Does yours smoke?

MARO: He smokes some.

FOTINI: Maybe he's just a follower ... a misguided follower. Because there is that category, you know, Aleka ... the misguided ones.

ALEKA: I don't know...

FOTINI: Unless of course he's a Nazi of such high rank, as to appear in the guise of a normal person. In which case, you simply throw in the towel.

MARO: He's not Fotini, he's not ... Misguided, perhaps ... But a high-ranking official no. It's not possible.

FOTINI: Say, where is he now?

MARO: He's sleeping ... He's expecting me to wake him up and make him coffee.

FOTINI: I'm really curious to meet him.

ALEKA: Well, I'm just letting you know. If I miss the chance to get Stefano back ... I'll go crazy! I'll go wandering off through the fields singing folk songs ... (*She cries.*)

MARO: (*in a sudden outburst*) I'm going to lose him, Aleka ... I'll lose him, I'm telling you...

ALEKA: You'll lose him in fifteen days?

MARO: I'll lose him ... I'll lose him...

ELECTRA: Don't worry. Those guys don't get lost so easily.

MARO: It's happened to me before, Electra. It's happened before...

ALEKA: Leave her alone, Electra ... Leave her alone ... I know my fate ... (*She cries.*)

MARO: My God, what's happening to us? What are we going through?

ALEKA: I know my fate...

(*Long pause*)

MARO: Wait a minute ... Hector is leaving for Luxembourg on Saturday ... He'll be back ... hold on ... Monday to Monday eight ... Tuesday nine, Wednesday ten ... Say I'm back the eleventh. Because if we leave the day after tomorrow I miss two days – that I would be with him ...

I'll make that sacrifice, as long as I'm here when he returns ... I'll miss two days now in order to be here then ... I have to be back on the eleventh.

ALEKA: For two days? All this for two days?

MARO: That's all I know. As soon as he sets foot here, on the eleventh. I want to be at the airport to meet him.

ALEKA: Is it so all important for chrissake?

MARO: You shouldn't want it all your way, Aleka ... You can't have it all your way ... When Hector arrives I want to be here.

ALEKA: (*thinking it over*) Well, all right...

MARO: And I have to see how I'm going to tell him now ... How I'm going to break it to him ... Because it will really upset him that I'm leaving the day after tomorrow ... (*To* FOTINI) You can't control yourself ... You simply have no control...

FOTINI: Go on now, you better leave ... When's the man going to drink his coffee?

MARO: Yes, I should go make his coffee.

ALEKA: Here, take him these chocolates pastries ... they're fresh.

MARO: Oh, that's nice.

FOTINI: Tell him these are from Aleka.

MARO: Oh, Aleka! (*She hugs her.*)

ALEKA: Go on ... (*She gives her the pastries.*)

MARO: That so nice. Well, I'm leaving now...

FOTINI: Tell him Fotini says hello.

MARO: OK, I will ... I have to stop off and get him his cigarettes ... (*She leaves.*)

ALEKA: Oh, my goodness! I'm in such a state ... I'm in a state of total confusion! So, what do I have to do now? ... Let's take things in order ... one by one ... A call to the travel agency to book tickets ... (*She goes to the telephone.*) By the way, Fotini ... Where will you be staying all that time?

FOTINI: All what time?

ALEKA: All the time we'll be gone. Because, of course, you won't be able to wander around the streets of Kifissia, window shopping...

FOTINI: Why can't I?

ALEKA: Didn't Anthony say the three of us would be going to Thailand? That you would come too.

FOTINI: So what if he did?

ALEKA: It has to look like you're gone too. Really, why didn't we think of that, Electra?

FOTINI: I said I'd go – I didn't go.

ALEKA: You're going to make Anthony out to be liar? If he comes out a liar, it's all over!

ELECTRA: (*to* F) You know, she's right...

ALEKA: We've blown the whole thing to pieces!

ELECTRA: Because Stefano will say. 'Is this all just another lie? Just another lie?'

ALEKA: My God, what a disaster!

FOTINI: Oh, come on I simply changed my mind. At the last moment I changed my mind.

ALEKA: That's absolutely out of the question! You have to disappear.

FOTINI: Disappear? How can I disappear?

ALEKA: Bank, cinema, restaurant kiosk for cigarettes – they're all prohibited.

FOTINI: What?

ALEKA: And your car must remain parked in the same spot at all times. No telephone, nothing. You must disappear from the face of the earth.

FOTINI: What are you saying?

ALEKA: Because if the slightest thing goes wrong and Stefano finds out that this was all set up ... you've destroyed me. Do you see Electra? If the slightest thing goes wrong she's destroyed me.

ELECTRA: She's destroyed you!

FOTINI: So what are you trying to tell me? That I'm obliged to shut myself up in my house?

ALEKA: There's no other way. You have to close yourself indoors. But where? Because your house, Maro's, Anthony's, and our house you can forget about. He's going to send his niece Christine around to every single one of our houses to investigate! And do you know

Christine at all? She'll call up your mother ... Oh my God! She'll follow Anthony ... Oh my God! All is lost. If Christine gets her hooks into us, we're done for! Oh, my God!

FOTINI: What can I do? Where can I go?

ALEKA: I don't know. I don't know ... Disappear. Get lost.

FOTINI: What do you mean get lost, Aleka? How can I get lost?

ALEKA: How should I know? Go to Anthony's summer house.

FOTINI: Go to Vivari?

ALEKA: Go to Vivari.

FOTINI: Alone? I can't stay alone for one minute. Me stay alone at Vivari? Fifteen days at Vivari ... Are you out of your minds? Of all places, Vivari ... Close myself up alone at Vivari...

ALEKA: Well, what do you suggest, then? What else do you suggest?

FOTINI: If I get chased by those owls...

(ELECTRA *laughs*.)

FOTINT: What? You think it's a joke? Last time these owls attacked, and I almost went crazy.

ALEKA: Owls? What owls?

FOTINI: These owls, Aleka ... Anthony had gone on an emergency call ... and owls came out of the vineyards...

ELEKTRA: No shit!

FOTINI: They saw the light ... I don't know what happened. And they came and perched in all the trees around the house, and they hooted at me. What if something like that happens again?

ALEKA: Well, where will you go then? What will you do?

FOTINI: I don't know what I'll do. But I'm certainly not going to Vivari. And I can't stay closed up inside.

ALEKA: Oh, my God? She'll give me away.

FOTINI: It's out of the question. Don't you even consider the possibility. There's no way I'll close myself up inside a house again.

ALEKA: She's going to give me away ... She's going to destroy me...

FOTINI: All you can think about is closing me up inside a house ... Locking me up ... Well just you listen here ... I have my limits too, I' m willing to make a sacrifice when there's a need for it, but up to a point. What do you want to do, drive me crazy? But I've had enough, thank you very much! How much do you think a person can stand? Do you think it takes a lot to drive someone crazy? Do you?

(*Pause*)

ALEKA: Fine. Then you'll come with me.

FOTINI: To Thailand? It's out of the question!

ALEKA: I'm not leaving you here, Fotini. You're coming with me. That's all there is to it.

FOTINI: In the first place, you don't want me. Isn't that what you said before? That you don't want me and you'll go with Maro? Well then, you just go with Maro.

ALEKA: I'll not hear another word. I'm not letting you stay here.

FOTINI: I can't come, Aleka, It's a question of dignity now.

ALEKA: But I see exactly what will happen. The telephone will ring ... you'll pick up the receiver ... you'll say hello ... and they'll hang up. Well, that is the moment my life ends forever!
And I'll end up in group therapy ... asking for understanding from people who are in despair...

(*Pause.* ALEKA *sits to one side, looking victimized.*)

FOTINI: So what do you want me to do? Do you want me to go wherever Anthony sends me?

ELECTRA: It beats sitting shut up in a house watching ghosts...

FOTINI: I can't do it. He has to be punished. So I can find a balance, understand?

ELECTRA: Can I tell you something?

FOTINI: No, there's nothing you can say.

ELECTRA: Just let me say one thing.

FOTINI: No, there's nothing you can say.

ELECTRA: Just let me say one thing.

FOTINI: Don't insist. I'm not backing down on this.

ELECTRA: Listen, you can settle the score with him afterwards.

FOTINI: Afterwards? What do you mean, afterwards?

ELECTRA: You'll go to Thailand now, you'll come back, he'll think he got his way, he'll calm down ... And one day, out of the blue, baaamm! You'll say 'Be back in a moment, I'm just going down for cigarettes,' and in three hours you'll be drinking coffee in Paris ... Where? But ... What? ... Who saw her? Nothing...

FOTINI: In Paris?

ELECTRA: You can drive him crazy. Isn't that what you want?

FOTINI: I like it...

ELECTRA: As soon as he thinks he's got everything under control ... bam, right on the head!

FOTINI: I really like it...

ELECTRA: And then you'll see how crazy Anthony can get ... I mean we're talking about really crazy.

FOTINI: I like it ... I really like it...

ALEKA: Fotini, my darling...

FOTINI: Hold on ... Give me a minute to think ... just one minute.

(*Pause*)

FOTINI: There's no other way. I have to come.

ALEKA: That's what I've been saying. You have to come.

FOTINI: Aleka, there's no way for me not to come. I have to come.

ALEKA: You have to come.

FOTINI: I have to come. Because look ... If I don't come, then you – regardless of what happens, will put the blame on me. Well, since that's the case, I'm coming.

ALEKA: That's all I want too. For you to come.

FOTINI: I'll come, Aleka. There's no way for me not to come.

ALEKA: My dear Fotini!

FOTINI: There's no way for me not to come...

ALEKA: (*hugs her*) Dear Fotini! My dear Fotini!

FOTINI: Because if I don't come ... (*Pause*) I'll come.

(ALEKA *collapses on the couch, exhausted and relieved.*)

FOTINI: And I'll settle the score with him afterwards.

ELECTRA: You'll let him have it afterwards ... (*To* ALEKA)
Well, go on now, book the tickets.

ALEKA: (*gets up*) Ah! The camera! Where have we put the
camera?

ELECTRA: How should I know? It's around somewhere.

ALEKA: What does that mean, it's around somewhere.

ELECTRA: Upstairs somewhere. Go look.

ALEKA: (*goes to look for it – stops*) And just how am I going
to face him?

ELECTRA: Who?

ALEKA: When I return from Thailand. If he looks me in the
eye and says: I'm asking you for the last time. Did you
sleep with the Maestro?

ELECTRA: You're going to face up to him.

ALEKA: Which means?

ELECTRA: You're going to say no.

ALEKA: Right, now I'm frightened ... For the first time...

ELECTRA: It's settled, you're going to answer no.

ALEKA: If I can just get a hold on myself ... (*She exits.*)

ELECTRA: Well, now he'll be hanging around here again ...
Bathrobe and high notes...

(*Pause*)

FOTINI: And who am I going to go with?

ELECTRA: Where?

FOTINI: To Paris. Alone?

ELECTRA: Why, is that a problem?

FOTINI: Because I will not travel alone...

ELECTRA: We'll go together.

FOTINI: Because alone I...

ELECTRA: As soon as we wrap up the filming, you and I

take off the very next day.

FOTINI: Because I can't depend on those two . . .

ELECTRA: Depend on me.

FOTINI: I can't trust them.

ELECTRA: I'm telling you we'll go together . . .

FOTINI: Well, if we go together . . .

ELECTRA: And if you want to know . . . I'm going to put one over on Jason. Because he needs a lesson too. Did you know he cut one of my scenes? He said, 'We have to cut back on expenses and he cut out a sequence that I'm in . . .'

FOTINI: Did he really? Well then, he has to pay too.

ELECTRA: He cut one of my scenes.

(Pause)

FOTINI: I haven't been to Paris in quite some time . . . We'll go to Montmartre for coffee . . .

ELECTRA: To Montmartre . . . wherever you say . . .

FOTINI: Unless you want to go to Martinique.

ELECTRA: Martinique?

FOTINI: I've had this thing for Martinique since I was small . . . My uncle had some stamps with the word Martinique on them . . . and there were these oxen with big horns . . . and black women in coloured dresses . . . with baskets on their heads . . .

ELECTRA: Say, do you by any chance wake up early when you travel?

FOTINI: Don't worry . . .

ELECTRA: And like to go running around, here and there . . . sightseeing . . . and stuff like that?

FOTINI: You call the shots, dear . . . Whatever you like . . .

ELECTRA: Actually I could go for sleeping on a riverboat . . .

FOTINI: Then we'll go to Egypt . . . There you get really sleepy. As soon as you set foot in Egypt you get sleepy . . . That's what I've been told . . .

ELECTRA: On the Nile . . . Great . . . But I would like a cup of coffee in Montmartre . . .

FOTINI: Also there are some out of the way places no one's ever heard of . . .

ELECTRA: We'll disappear just like that...

FOTINI: Just like that!

ELECTRA: And we will never ever tell anyone! Not about where we went, what we did ... nothing!

FOTINI: We'll get away from those two as well...

ELECTRA: From them as well...

FOTINI: Like that!

ELECTRA: Like that! And we will keep it a secret forever ... One point in our lives cloaked in mystery, hidden from all...

FOTINI: It's wonderfully evil!

ELECTRA: Can you keep a secret like that? Because you can get carried away without warning and...

FOTINI: You have nothing to worry about ... nothing...

ELECTRA: Because this is one of those secrets where, say, ten years from now ... and airplane is falling and you're in it and you have no chance whatever of surviving ... because the airplane is falling from three thousand metres straight down over cement...

FOTINI: Cement?

ELECTRA: ...And you know that soon you're gonna be wiped out...

FOTINI: What are you saying?

ELECTRA: ...And you have but a few seconds left to live ... and Jason says to you and my mother says to you, and Anthony says to you ... 'Tell us, for God's sake, where did you two go that time you suddenly disappeared What did you do?' You will say nothing!

FOTINI: Nothing!

ELECTRA: Are you resolved to keeping this secret forever?

FOTINI: I am, Electra my dear, I am!

ELECTRA: And let the plane fall?

FOTINI: That's a bit morbid...

ELECTRA: And let it fall?

FOTINI: Let it fall, let it fall...

The End

About the Authors

Loula Anagnostaki

Loula Anagnostaki casts her eye over the range of human relationships. This is fertile soil and she digs deep exposing the inner life of her characters. With scrupulous honesty, the complexities, contradictions and paradoxes of the human condition are writ large on stage. Uncomfortable maybe, but the openness of her characters means that they continually break new ground.

For Anagnostaki theatre must be more than merely entertainment; the mind must be animated, the audience involved. Central to the playwright is the conviction that the audience take something integral away with them. Anything less and the audience is short-changed.

Plays by Loula Anagnostaki:
Staying Overnight – The City – The Parade: three one-act plays first performed in 1965 by the Athens Art Theatre.
Staying Overnight has been screened on Cyprus TV. *The City* was performed in Padova, Italy by Teatro dei Verdi. In Britain, it was staged by the Soho Theatre Company and aired by the BBC, directed by Martin Esslin. *The Parade* was staged in France (1969) and Italy under the direction of Antoine Vitez. It was performed in Bonn, Germany in the mid 1980s and the Theatre Lab Company (1997) first staged it in Britain.
Associating was first performed in 1967 by the National Theatre of Greece.
Antonio or the Message was first performed in 1970 by the Athens Art Theatre.
The Victory was first staged in 1978 by the Athens Art Theatre.
The Cassette was first performed in 1982 by the Athens Art Theatre.
The Sound of The Gun was first performed in 1987 by the Athens Art Theatre.
Diamonds and Blues was first performed in 1991 by Theatro Karezi.
The Trip Away was first performed in 1996 by the Athens Art Theatre.
The Sky Deep Red was first performed in 1998 by the National Theatre of Greece.

Eleni Haviara

Eleni Haviara was born and brought up in Egypt. She studied drama
and English literature in Athens. An actress until 1970, she has since
taught English literature at the University of Athens. Her work in
theatre includes the monograph *Acting by Gender: Women in Arthur
Miller's Dramaturgy* (1991) and the plays *The Laurels and the Bitter
Laurels* and *With Power from Kifissia*, in collaboration with Dimitris
Kehaidis.

Dimitris Kehaidis

Dimitris Kehaidis was born and brought up in Greece. While studying
Law at university he wrote his first one-act plays, *Long Sad Song*
(1957), *Games in the saltmarshes* (1957) and *The Long Walk* (1959), all
performed by the Athens Art Theatre.
Suburb of Neo Faliro was first shown by Greek TV in 1960.
The Public Feast was first performed in 1964 by the Athens Art
Theatre.
The Wedding Ring and *Backgammon* were first performed in 1972 by
the Athens Art Theatre.
The Laurels and the Bitter Laurels (in collaboration with Eleni Haviara)
was first performed in 1979 by the Athens Art Theatre. *With Power
From Kifissia*, (in collaboration with Eleni Haviara) was first performed
in 1995 by New Stage.
  His plays has been performed abroad and also presented by BBC
Radio 3 and DDR.